Collins

need to know?

Dog and Puppy Care

Collins

First published in 2007 by Collins
an imprint of
HarperCollins Publishers
77–85 Fulham Palace Road
London W6 8JB

www.collins.co.uk

Collins is a registered trademark of HarperCollins Publishers Limited

11 10 09 08 07
6 5 4 3 2 1

A catalogue record for this book is available from the British Library

Editor: Heather Thomas
Designer: Rolando Ugolini
Series design: Mark Thomson
Photographers: Rolando Ugolini, Charlie Colmer, David Dalton and
Bruce Tanner
Front cover photograph: © bilderlounge/Alamy
Back cover photographs: Rolando Ugolini

Based on material from *The Family Dog*

ISBN-13: 978 0 00 723295 6
ISBN-10: 0 00 723295 0

Colour reproduction by Colourscan, Singapore
Printed and bound by Printing Express Lt

Contents

Introduction 6

1 **Choosing a dog** 8

2 **The new puppy** 22

3 **The adult dog** 58

4 **Training your dog** 82

5 **Good dog behaviour** 102

6 **The healthy dog** 138

Need to know more? 188

Index 190

Introduction

Over the centuries the dog has become 'Man's best friend' and an increasing number of people own dogs for companionship. Most of today's breeds evolved as working dogs with specific functions from their common ancestor – the wolf.

Whichever breed of dog you own, he will become your loyal friend and companion for many years to come, and you must take your responsibilities seriously.

The human-canine pack

Living in a human-canine pack can be a rewarding experience for both the owner and the dog. You will need to look after your dog and provide for both his mental and physical welfare as well as developing an understanding of his behaviour and body language if you are to become a responsible owner. Your dog must learn to adapt to family life if he is to grow into a well-behaved member of your 'pack'.

Dogs are truly amazing and adaptable animals. As well as being our loyal companions, they are valued co-workers – flushing out gamebirds, guarding our homes and livestock, sniffing out contraband drugs and explosives or even delectable truffles, rescuing people on mountains and in earthquakes, or simply visiting the sick and elderly in hospitals to lower their blood pressure and speed up their recovery.

It is not only a privilege and a pleasure to own a dog but also a responsibility which you should take very seriously – a dog is for life and he will become your trusted companion and confidant. Like in any relationship, you both need to work at building a successful partnership. This book will help you to understand your dog better, to care for him in a responsible way and to enjoy owning a well-behaved friend with whom you can spend many happy years.

1 Choosing a dog

Buying a dog is a huge responsibility and one
of the most important decisions that any owner
will have to make. A dog is for life and he will
become your responsibility for at least the next
ten years and therefore you should not rush into
getting one without considering how he will fit
into your lifestyle and what you can give him
in return. Owning a dog is extremely rewarding
but your furry friend will need regular exercise,
feeding, grooming and companionship, and
you must be prepared to set aside some time
every day to care for him and play with him.

Getting a pedigree dog

Buying a puppy or an adult dog is one of the most important purchases of a lifetime. You will be assuming control of another creature's life and you are, in effect, buying a new member of the family. But what sort of dog should you buy?

Opposite: Both Labradors and Retrievers make good family pets. They are highly biddable, very easy to train and love to be around people. However, they do need a lot of exercise.

A family decision
Because it is such an important decision, it is a good idea to consult your family, from the youngest to the eldest, for every one will bear some responsibility in different areas of the dog's life. Children should be closely involved as the lessons they learn from dog ownership now will help them to be more caring to animals and humans later on in their adult life.

Which breed?
There is a breed of dog that is suitable for every one. The UK Kennel Club registers over 170 breeds and although it will take some research to discover which one is ideal for you, all the effort will be worthwhile. Your first consideration is where you live and the size and style of your home. All dogs love freedom and are suitable for country living, with the exception of only some very small heavy-coated breeds, but not all dogs are suited to city life. It would be wrong to condemn a large dog, such as a St Bernard, Great Dane or any of the large Hounds, to life in a small inner-city apartment, but dogs, being what they are, would learn to adapt to the life. However, the fact remains that it would not be fair and would almost certainly lead to problems, particularly regarding the dog's behaviour and temperament.

Owning a dog can be rewarding and you will receive many happy years of companionship and affection from your canine pals. Stroking and playing with dogs reduces stress in many people.

Consider your lifestyle

If you live in a development where houses are quite close together, your neighbours must be respected. They have the right to peace and quiet, and a breed that is inclined to yap or bark is not suitable. Nor do you want a breed that has the reputation of being aggressive to other dogs and too defensive of its owner. Unfortunately, not everyone likes dogs, and therefore it is not wise to introduce an element into your life which will bring unnecessary aggravation.

Next, consider your own attitudes; if you are a very tidy person, a dog with a thick double coat which tends to moult heavily would soon become a source of irritation. He would require daily grooming but would you have the time to do this?

There are other considerations, too, concerning your lifestyle. Do you work and are you away from the house for long periods? Is a member of the family willing and able to walk the dog at least twice a day? Who will be responsible for feeding him and making sure that fresh water is always available? Have you considered the costs of owning a dog? There will not only be food to buy but also equipment such as bedding, bowls, a collar and lead, toys and treats, not to mention vet's bills, pet insurance and fees for training and socialization classes if you get a puppy rather than an adult dog.

The right breed for you

Breed	Temperament
Labrador Retriever	Affable, tolerant and easy-going with dogs and humans. Easily trained and learns quickly. Enjoys the company of children. A superb family and working dog.
Golden Retriever	Gentle, biddable and highly intelligent. A good working dog and an excellent family pet. Good with children and a great companion and gundog.
Rottweiler	Intensely protective and highly intelligent, this is a good guarding breed. Needs good socialization and kind but firm training. Not to be left with young children.
German Shepherd Dog	Highly intelligent and a wonderful guarding and working dog, the German Shepherd makes a good family pet if it is trained and well-socialized. Needs kind but firm handling.
Parson Jack Russell Terrier	Intelligent, alert and always busy, this dog loves to hunt. An easily trained fun dog that loves to live within its family pack and is usually good with children. Affectionate and a watchful guard dog.
Cavalier King Charles Spaniel	A gentle, docile and intelligent little dog. Confident and fun-loving with a friendly nature, the Cavalier King Charles makes a good family pet and loves to play with children if they are not too rough.
Boxer	Exuberant, full of fun, loyal and affectionate. A good guard dog and a loving family dog. Good with children but can be over-boisterous with very young ones.
Yorkshire Terrier	Playful, inquisitive, a good companion and the perfect small pet, especially for the elderly. A spirited, game little dog who enjoys hunting and playing games.
English Springer Spaniel	Gentle, loving and good with children. Craves affection and hates to be left alone. Highly intelligent and easy to train. A loving family pet as well as a good working dog. Needs a lot of exercise.
Cocker Spaniel	Gentle, intelligent, biddable and easily trained. A good companion and family dog, especially with children. A happy working dog, good at retrieving.
Poodle	Highly sensitive, loving and intelligent, the Poodle can be easily trained and makes a delightful family pet. It is gentle with children and a good companion for all ages.
Dalmatian	Affectionate, anxious to please and loves human company. Devoted, loyal and very attached to children. A dog that is more suited to country than town life.
Dobermann	Loyal, affectionate, intelligent and easily trained. Its power must be controlled and it needs kind but firm treatment. Not to be left with young children.
West Highland White Terrier	Intelligent, inquisitive and mischievous with an independent spirit. A good family dog which loves to be involved in every activity. Relatively easy to train.

Pedigree puppies

You may opt to start from scratch and to buy a pedigree puppy.
If you have done your research, you will have probably worked
out a shortlist of two or three breeds you like and which will fit
into your lifestyle. You should now try to find a suitable breeder.

must know

Which sex?
Choosing between a dog
and a bitch is not easy.
Bitches are presumed
to be gentler and more
biddable, but many
owners claim that dogs
are more sensitive. The
problem with bitches
is that they come into
season every six to nine
months and must be
kept away from males
or puppies will ensue.
Spaying the bitch and
castrating the male
prevents the problem
and does not affect the
character of either.

Finding a breeder

The best place to contact breeders is at a dog show,
but many of the minority breeds are quite scarce and
you may have to go on a waiting list for a puppy. The
choice of breeder is really important, so if you don't
like him or her do not buy a puppy from them. The
ideal breeder has a policy of breeding sound dogs,
both mentally and physically, will take advantage
of all the modern veterinary technology as far as
genetic tests are concerned, and will be interested
in the puppy's future life. Be prepared for some
searching questions about your lifestyle, and, in
return, a good breeder will not be offended if you
ask leading questions about their breeding history.

Genetic tests

From your research, you will know which, if any,
genetic anomalies affect your favourite breeds.
One of the most frequent in the larger dogs is hip
dysplasia. The best breeders have been working on
this problem for many years and are succeeding in
reducing the incidence in most breeds. You should
have found out the average score for the breed and
the breeder will show you either the parents' scores
or the mother's British Veterinary Association/
Kennel Club score sheet. If the score is very much

higher than the norm, you would be well advised not to buy one of the puppies, however cute. There are other genetic tests, particularly for eye conditions that affect some breeds. The Kennel Club will be happy to advise you about any genetic abnormalities that may be present in different breeds.

Choosing a puppy

Take your family to see the puppies, which should be over eight weeks old when they leave their mother, but make sure the children are under control. If the puppies have not encountered children before, they might be disturbed by them. Always ask to view the puppies' mother. This will enable you not only to see the fully-grown size of an adult dog but also, and more importantly, to judge her temperament.

Whichever sex you have decided upon, ask the breeder to remove the others and then examine the puppies individually. Look for any sort of discharge from the eyes, the mouth, the anus or the vulva; if any is present, don't take that puppy. The runt of the litter should also be discounted. On no account, be persuaded to buy a puppy at a lower price because 'there is something minor wrong with it'. Therein lies trouble. If everything looks good, then watch for the most extrovert puppy: the one that approaches you boldly, full of curiosity and happiness. Harden your heart and ignore any puppies that creep about apprehensively.

You should never buy a puppy without seeing the mother first. This will help you assess a pup's eventual size, appearance and temperament.

Where to buy

There are many traps into which potential owners can fall, so beware. Selling puppies and young dogs is now a multi-million pound business, and unfortunately there are a few unscrupulous breeders, dealers and retailers waiting for the gullible buyer.

Buy from breeders or charities

Most people have heard or read about 'puppy farms'. However, these are not farms in the true sense of the word but premises on which puppies are bred with no thought to their welfare, physically or mentally. They are fed on cheap and inferior foods with no veterinary attention or socialization (see page 40). They are bred purely for profit and their breeders are not concerned where they go or what happens to them after they leave their premises. The puppies may be sold direct to the public via misrepresented newspaper advertisements or they may go to dealers who will sell them by any method. Alternatively, they may be sold on through pet shops.

It must be emphasized that these puppies do not have a good future, and it is most unlikely that the vendors will offer a 'back-up' or that a puppy can be returned if it develops any problems. Therefore it is always wise to buy a puppy direct from a breeder, who should be recognized by the Kennel Club, or from a registered charity.

Go on the Internet and log onto the Kennel Club's website for a list of breed clubs and breeders. Many breed societies run their own rescue organizations to find good homes for unwanted dogs or pets who have been ill-treated or their owners have died.

Getting a mongrel

Before you opt for an expensive pedigree dog, why not consider getting a mongrel instead? They are just as lovable, often more healthy, and you will be giving a puppy or an adult rescue dog the opportunity of a good home and loving family.

Advantages and disadvantages

Some people claim that pedigree dogs are less healthy than mongrels or cross-breeds, but although this may be true of a few breeds, it cannot be proven generally. There are two reasons why a pedigree dog is a pedigree: his ancestry is known and recorded; and he breeds true, i.e. if you mate a dog and a bitch of one breed the puppies produced will be replicas of their parents (colour excepted). Because mongrels come from a much greater gene pool, they have less inherited health problems than pure-bred dogs.

One of the advantages of a pedigree is that you will know the size to which he will grow and the sort of temperament he will develop. Getting a mongrel is a bit of a lottery – unless you have background knowledge about his parents, a cute little creature at eight weeks might grow into a giant at 18 months. There is also the risk that he may inherit some nasty genes from one parent which may not manifest themselves until he is an adult, so there are risks involved.

However, with cross-breeds, you may know quite a lot about a puppy's pure-bred parents and, with the breed characteristics of both sides, the chances are that he will grow up into a loving, well-behaved family pet. Every mongrel is unique with its own individual character and looks.

No matter what sort of dog you choose, a pedigree or a mongrel, he can enrich your life and will become part of your family.

Rescue dogs

Not everyone wants the hard work and problems associated with rearing a puppy, and may prefer an adult or a rescue dog. A network of breed rescue organizations exists to help you, and a call to the Kennel Club will provide the information you need.

must know

National charities
Both Battersea Dogs' Home and the Dogs Trust give dogs of all breeds, including abandoned mongrels, the chance of a new life by re-training them, treating their ailments and matching them very carefully with potential owners. You can return a dog who fails to fit into his new home; further efforts will be made to re-home him, no matter how long it takes.

Opposite: A rescue dog, like this Lurcher, can make a loyal and loving pet, who will be just as rewarding as a pedigree dog.

Reasons for rescue

There are many reasons for dogs to be in rescue: broken marriages, deaths or owners going overseas to live. Many of these dogs come from happy homes, are well-trained and can adapt to life in any caring family. However, some have been ill treated and will require tender loving care before they feel confident in their new home. Because of this, potential owners should be prepared for some searching questions before the dog is handed over. You may have to pay a small fee to cover expenses.

Rescuing a Greyhound

Of all pedigree dogs, Greyhounds have the biggest problem. Many racing Greyhounds are bred in Britain and the Irish Republic – far too many dogs for the market to absorb – and, as a result, numerous Greyhounds are abandoned by callous owners if they don't make the grade. These gentle dogs can be trained not to chase small furry animals and can make extremely loving companions and good family pets. There are specialist rescue organizations for the breed, which not only rehome ex-racers but actually go to the race tracks in Spain (where Greyhounds are frequently ill treated) and buy them back. These dogs are then re-homed in Britain (see page 188).

Assessing a rescue dog

When you see a dog you like, interact with him and then run through a few simple tasks to observe his reaction to you and how he behaves in different situations, both with other dogs and with people.

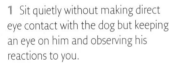

1 Sit quietly without making direct eye contact with the dog but keeping an eye on him and observing his reactions to you.

2 Offer him a small treat or piece of food and watch his reaction. Does he snatch it greedily, regard it suspiciously or refuse to eat it?

3 Ask the staff at the rescue centre whether you can observe the dog's behaviour when he is mixing with other dogs.

4 Put a lead on the dog and take him for a walk. Note how he reacts to you. Put him back in the kennel and invite him out again.

Choosing a rescue dog

When you are looking for a rescue dog, the main problem is the beguiling eyes of the dogs. Every one will touch your heart but you must be practical. Make sure you decide on the size of dog you want and how much time you are prepared to spend on exercising him and grooming his coat before you go along to a rescue centre to look for one.

Talk to the staff

It is in the interests of the staff to find permanent homes and to match you with a suitable dog, so listen carefully to their advice before choosing a particular dog. Speak to the person who normally walks the dog that interests you, and ask them about his temperament, obedience and willingness to please, how energetic he is and how he gets on with people and other dogs.

Choose a friendly, responsive dog

The dog may be suspicious of you initially, but don't worry – this is natural. He should come to you after about five minutes. However, if he shows any signs of aggression, then beware. If he lies on his back urinating slightly, he is being submissive, and although this is acceptable in puppies it is not desirable in adult dogs. However appealing these dogs may look, harden your heart and walk away. Taking on a rescue dog is inevitably a bit of a gamble because his history is usually unknown, but he is more likely to settle into his new home and become a much-loved member of your family if he is friendly and responsive. When you take him home with you, be patient and give him lots of your time.

want to know more?

• To find out which breed of dog is right for you and source a responsible breeder of pedigree dogs, check out The Kennel Club's website: www.the-kennel-club. org.uk
• For a comprehensive guide to rehoming and rescue centres, go to: www.animalrescuers. co.uk

weblinks

• To rehome a rescue dog, contact one of the following charities: Battersea Dogs' Home at www.dogshome.org or the Dogs Trust at www.dogstrust.org.uk or the National Animal Welfare Trust at www.nawt.org.uk

2 The new puppy

A puppy's experiences and socialization in his
first year are very important and influence the
sort of adult he will grow into. The best time to
collect your puppy is when he is between eight
and nine weeks old. At this age, he should be
mature enough to settle into a new home with
minimal stress for both of you. Start socializing
him and introduce him to all the scents, sounds,
objects and experiences that will be part of his
everyday life. Learning about the world will help
to make your puppy more confident and less
likely to have behaviour problems later on.

The perfect puppy

Having made the momentous decision to get a puppy, you need to plan for his arrival in your home. With the help of children and other family members, you can decide on which equipment and toys your new puppy will need and buy them before he arrives.

Equipment

The canine magazines are full of advertisements for suitable accessories, but if you are lucky, there might be a really good pet shop close by to point you in the right direction. Your puppy will need some essential items of equipment, including a soft puppy collar and a lead, feeding and water bowls, grooming tools (depending on his coat type), some bedding and a bed, as well as some strong toys and suitable hide chews on which to chew, especially while he is teething. You will also need to get in some food in advance – find out from the breeder what he has been fed and ask for a diet sheet to help you plan out his meals as he gets older, and as a guide to the correct quantities to feed him.

Opposite and right: Choosing a puppy is never an easy task as they all look appealing, but you must harden your heart and not be tempted to take more than one.

Settling your puppy in

The first thing to impress on everybody in your family is that the puppy should not be taken into a public place before having his course of vaccinations for fear of infection (see page 50). Give him a name but only use it with pleasant connotations.

(see page 50)

must know

Good manners
It's never too early to start encouraging your puppy to behave well. By preventing unwanted behaviour now, you are setting down guidelines for the future and the puppy will be less likely to develop behavioural problems. Reward good behaviour with a treat, a stroke and praise, and discourage or stop any problem behaviour, such as begging for food while you're eating, jumping up at visitors, barking excessively or growling.

A safe refuge

Provide a place for your puppy that he can call his own – a warm, draught-free corner of the kitchen is ideal. You can invest in a soft, washable bed or a hard, unchewable plastic bed lined with soft bedding or machine-washable, fleecy man-made fabric, but this is not strictly necessary at this stage.

When puppies are very young, they often have a great liking for cardboard boxes, so try turning a box upside-down, cutting an entry hole in it and putting in an old sweater. Your puppy will love it because he feels safe inside. He can chew the box and it can be renewed at no expense. When he gets older, you can buy a proper chew-proof dog bed of adequate size.

Whenever he goes into his box, leave him in peace. Instruct your children that his bed is his private sanctuary and he must be allowed to sleep without being disturbed. Like a young child, a puppy needs rest. It is during these periods that his body and bones develop and grow. Whenever you put the puppy in his box, give him the command 'In your bed' and he will soon understand what you mean.

Playpens
Many people find that a puppy playpen is a very good idea. It will keep your puppy safe and out of the way

of the children and family for short periods when you are busy and cannot keep an eye on him, while still allowing him to be with you all and to observe what is going on around him. Place the puppy's box inside the playpen, together with his toys and chews, and cover the floor with newspapers in case of accidents. The puppy can rest, sleep or play inside, and the playpen can be moved from room to room. Don't leave him in the playpen for too long, however.

The first two days

During this period, do not hassle the puppy – let him investigate his new home in his own time. Comfort and reassure him because he will feel lonely and will miss his littermates and mother. Don't leave him alone in the house but be with him, talking to him and playing gently with him. This is an important socialization period and what you do now will set the pattern for your future relationship.

Don't give the puppy any sweets and 'treats' or he may get an upset stomach. Leave a bowl of fresh water down for him, topping up the water or changing it on a regular basis, and give him the food he is used to eating to avoid any digestive problems.

Puppies enjoy chewing expensive baskets and plastic beds, so a cardboard box may be a cheaper and more practical alternative. If your puppy chews it, just throw it away and get a new one.

Feeding your puppy

The breeder should give you a diet sheet together with a small supply of the food on which your puppy has been weaned. To avoid any problems, stick to the regime as closely as possible.

Feeding guidelines

Puppies have tiny stomachs and should be fed only small amounts frequently – as many as four or five meals a day. After two or three weeks, you can reduce the number of meals to three and slightly increase the amounts given at each meal. Every breed will differ but by the time your puppy is five to six months old, he should be eating two meals a day. Always feed the best food possible, at the same time and in the same place to establish a routine. A wide range of specially formulated puppy food is available, including complete dried foods, canned foods, biscuit meal and mixers. Alternatively, cook fresh meat and mix it with special puppy biscuit meal.

A puppy needs small, regular meals while he is very young. A bowl of fresh water should always be available.

A nutritious diet

It is impossible to over-estimate the importance of giving a dog the correct food. There are hundreds of brands from which to choose and you need to find out which suits your puppy best. The advantage of modern commercial puppy foods is that they provide the right scientific balance of essential nutrients for a growing dog, and there should be no need for vitamin or mineral supplements, unless your vet recommends them. Whatever food you offer, an unlimited amount of fresh water must be available.

How much and how often?

Puppies have incredibly small stomachs and after weaning they need small feeds frequently: four or

Puppies need special foods that are formulated for their digestive systems – dried or canned.

Feed your puppy at regular times throughout the day.

Fresh food
If you don't want to feed convenience foods, you can give your puppy fish, meat or chicken mixed with rice, pasta, some mixer biscuit meal and vegetables. It's important to get the balance right, so ask your vet for advice. Some owners believe fresh food is healthier for their dogs and helps prevent behavioural problems. Check the labels on cans and boxes of dog food for additives.

If puppies eat together from the same bowl, make sure that each one is getting enough food.

five meals a day plus two puppy milk drinks. There is no way to know exactly how much to feed a puppy as every breed differs. A general guide, using complete puppy food, is 22g ($^3/_4$oz) per 450g (1lb) body weight daily, bearing in mind that medium-sized dogs will double their birth weight once every seven days, and larger dogs grow even faster. Every major specialist dog food manufacturing company gives guidelines, and most have a telephone helpline. The breeder or your vet can also advise you. The best way to monitor progress is to weigh the puppy daily. Any standstill or loss of weight needs immediate investigation, so make sure he is getting his proper quota and slightly increase the amount given if necessary.

Getting the portion size right
Always pay special attention to the manufacturers' recommendations and be sure not to overfeed your puppy. Dogs are running creatures and should be slim with hard muscles. Even small dogs, such as Pekingeses, should not carry any excess weight. If you are unsure about how much food your pup should be eating, then ask your vet for advice.

Feeding tips

- It is always very unwise to feed your puppy titbits from the table. If you don't start now when he's young, he will not bother you later on when you are eating.
- Don't offer the puppy sweets, cakes, sugar-based biscuits and chocolate. He will eat them but they are bad for his teeth and his weight.
- If your puppy does not eat his food immediately, don't leave it down for long in case insects contaminate it.
- Don't allow him to eat the cat's food or milk, nor should you feed them together.
- Don't feed the pup cow's milk while he is still very young. Some dogs react unfavourably to it and it may cause diarrhoea. All he needs is water to prosper.
- If he has a diet of complete dried food he will need lots of water, so make sure he has a continuous supply and change it frequently.
- If you introduce any new foods, always do this gradually, so as not to upset his stomach.

- Don't give your puppy cooked chicken, lamb or pork bones as these can splinter and cause serious injury. Hide chews will help with teething and cleaning teeth.
- Large knuckle bones can be given but train your pup to give them up to you to prevent him getting over-protective of food and treats. Do not let him have them for too long as he may chew off small pieces which could become impacted in his stomach.

Night-time

Missing the comforting presence of his fellow littermates, your puppy may cry during the first few nights in his new home, so try to tire him out by playing with him before he goes to sleep.

Comfort and safety

To keep your puppy warm, you can place a hot water bottle under his bedding. Some owners put a ticking clock in the same room and play the radio quietly, to fool the puppy into believing that he is not alone.

It is best to place his bed or box on a washable, non-carpeted floor and surround it with sheets of newspaper in case he wants to urinate during the night – puppies rarely soil their bed.

Crying at night

If your puppy howls during the night and you go to him, he will think you are answering his call and this may set a pattern for the future, so steel your heart and try not to go. Of course, he may need to go to the toilet outside. If you think this is the case, get up and take him out into the garden, waiting with him until he does something and then praising him.

It is cruel to let a puppy cry all night long and if he is very persistent and anxious and cannot settle, you may have to resort to bringing him into your bedroom for the first few nights. Put his box beside your bed and comfort him by stroking him from the bed. On no account should you let him get up onto the bed because this may encourage bad habits which will be very difficult to change when he grows to his full adult size.

Keeping the puppy safe

When the puppy gets more relaxed, you can move his box a little closer to the door each night until it is outside, and then it can be taken back to the kitchen. He will soon get used to being on his own in his bed as he becomes more confident in his new home and surroundings.

However, if he does sleep upstairs, make sure that he cannot fall downstairs – his bones will not calcify until he is about six months old and they can break quite easily at this age.

As a temporary precaution, you could try placing a child-proof stair gate at the top of the staircase at night. This can be used at the bottom of the stairs during the day to prevent the puppy from climbing upstairs. If he does go with you, always carry him up and down while he is small as he is likely to injure himself if he falls.

Provide your puppy with a snug bed that he can call his own. Make it comfortable with some soft washable rugs or 'vetbed'. If you buy a plastic basket for your puppy, get a suitable size for a fully-grown adult dog

House-training

Every puppy can be house-trained successfully, although some take longer to learn than others. By spending time with your dog and being patient, you can speed up the process and he will soon want to go outside in the garden rather than in the house.

When a puppy awakes from sleep and straight after feeding are good times to take him outside to be clean. Be patient! In the end, the penny will drop!

Territory marking

Toilet training is probably the subject that warrants priority in most households. However, it can be the most difficult attribute to teach; every puppy varies in his ability to grasp what it is that you want done because to the dog there are many in-built facets in the acts of urination and defecation. Territory marking is important to both dogs and bitches, as is pack-marking – eliminating on the same patch as that used by other dogs of the same breed or the same family. Male dogs do not usually use the leg-lifting marking stance for urination until they reach puberty, perhaps at 12 to 18 months old. Bitches usually squat to urinate all their lives but they may also lift a leg sometimes, especially when marking.

Pick a spot

When you first bring your puppy home, carry him into the garden and put him down on the patch that you would like to be used for elimination purposes. Try to pick somewhere near the house, as you will be spending quite a lot of time there! You may decide that paving is most easily cleaned, or you may want him to use the grass. Remember that on clay soil bitch urine bleaches the grass in circles, but on chalk soil this is not noticeable.

Your puppy will be anxious to urinate after the journey and so you will get a successful result almost straight away. Now praise your puppy exuberantly for his good behaviour before taking him inside.

You have to watch your puppy carefully to prevent him soiling in the house. Always keep the doors to your formal rooms shut unless you are actually in them, so the puppy does not have the opportunity to 'mess all over the house', as complaining owners say. Establish the times when you will take him outside, such as first thing in the morning, when he wakes up from a daytime sleep, straight away after feeding or drinking, following a vigorous game or play session, and before settling him down for the night. It is also a good idea to take him out after any excitement, such as when you have visitors or a family member returns home from work or shopping and is greeted enthusiastically by the puppy.

Taking your puppy out

You will need to take your puppy out regularly if you want him to be clean inside your home, and the emphasis is on taking him outside yourself. This means that you go too, rain or shine! It is absolutely useless to push the puppy outside, then close the door and leave him to his own devices. He will not be learning anything, except perhaps to wonder why he was suddenly shoved out into the cold. Go with your puppy – every hour on the hour if necessary. Stay near the place you have selected for him to use and say the words you have chosen to encourage him to perform – always use the same one or two words so that he will soon learn to recognize them. Praise and reward him rapturously when he goes.

must know

Be patient
House-training can take time, and its success depends on watching the puppy for tell-tale signs of his needs. Some breeds are quicker to learn than others – the smaller toy breeds are notoriously slow – but puppies are easier to train than babies. They don't urinate during sleep after four weeks of age whereas a child will not be dry overnight until it is four years old. Most puppies are house-trained by the time they are seven months old although the human child takes four years to reach this stage.

No garden?
If your house has not got a garden or you live in an apartment, you will have to choose a spot near your home to take your puppy to relieve himself. Pop some polythene bags in your pocket for picking up his mess, and then dispose of them safely and properly.

Using newspaper

At night or if the weather is bad and the puppy is very small, you can use newspaper. Although it only postpones the ordeal of garden training until later on, this system can be helpful in really cold, wet weather. To train your puppy to use the newspaper, place some thick pads near the door opening out into the garden. When he starts running backwards and forwards sniffing or turning round in small circles, pick him up and place him on the newspaper.

When he is accustomed to using the paper, you can gradually remove some pieces and then move the remainder towards the kitchen door. At the door it is then an easy matter to place the newspaper outside. At bedtime or if you are leaving the puppy for a short time in a playpen, you can surround his bed with sheets of newspaper in case of accidents. Instinctively, he will not want to soil his own nest.

Accidents will happen

If you do have the odd accident in the house, clean it up as soon as possible with a solution of biological washing powder to remove the smell. Dogs tend to return to the same spot if they can smell any traces of previous urination or defecation.

It may be a good idea, especially during any periods of cold, wet weather, to train your puppy to urinate on pads of newspaper.

Worth the time and effort

It takes time but, when learnt, house-training is there for a dog's life, except perhaps in illness or old age. Never chastise your puppy when he makes a mistake in the house unless you catch him in the act. If so, use your voice, never your hand. He regards urinating and defecating, and where he wants to do them, as perfectly normal behaviour and will not understand why you are punishing him. However, by taking him outside and praising him when he does go, he should soon relate the praise and reward to the required performance and will start asking you to go out. If he barks to attract your attention and runs to the door or paws at it, take him outside immediately and reward him when he goes.

Encourage your puppy to go out into the garden to urinate and defecate, whatever the weather. Walk round with him, watching until you are sure that he has relieved himself. Praise him profusely when he does so.

Introducing other pets

If you have other pets, you will need to introduce your puppy to them gradually, under your watchful instruction. Never leave them alone together – you must be present all the time.

Meeting cats

Do not force your new puppy to accept a resident cat. The socialization process will take time as they get accustomed to each other. Holding the cat near the puppy so he can smell it is not advisable – the cat will object and it could be painful for the puppy if he gets scratched. The cat will probably find a high place to stay safely out of the way for the first few days.

Feed them in different places and don't let the new puppy eat the cat's food; it may upset his stomach. Sooner or later the cat will venture out, but if the puppy gets too frisky the cat will defend itself. The puppy will soon learn to keep out of the cat's way.

Dogs and cats can become accustomed to each other and learn to live happily together, even sharing the same bed and playing games.

This Spaniel puppy is being introduced to a pet guinea pig. Neither animal seems stressed by the encounter but never leave your dog alone with a small pet.

In the fullness of time, it is usual for a dog and a cat to live together harmoniously in the same house, even after what might have been a tense start to their relationship. Some cats and dogs even sleep together in the same bed. However, this does not mean that the dog will tolerate a strange cat running across the lawn, and he may well chase it.

Small pets

Take special care to separate or even shield the new puppy from any pet rabbits, gerbils, hamsters, mice, guinea pigs or other small animals you may own, as they are a natural prey for a dog and it would be wise not to tempt him. When your puppy is a little older, he can be introduced to them but only under your supervision. Above all, you must make sure that he cannot follow his natural instincts and chase them, or frighten them with his presence. Most dogs will learn to live alongside small pets but it may take some time, and some breeds, such as terriers and sight hounds, may never accept the co-existence of smaller animals within the same household.

must know

Meeting other dogs
It is an important part of a puppy's socialization to meet other dogs from outside the family. This process can start at puppy classes where your dog will have the opportunity to meet and play with unfamiliar dogs of different breeds. This helps avoid problem encounters and possible fights in the future, and enables puppies to play together confidently. Your puppy will also have to meet adult dogs who are well-socialized.

Socializing your puppy

When a puppy faces something or someone whom he has never encountered before his first instinct is to run, and it is up to you, his owner, to socialize him so that he becomes accustomed to different people, other animals, traffic and loud noises.

If friends come to visit with their dogs, encourage them to handle and play with the new puppy.

Benefits of socialization

Inadequate socialization can lead to a puppy growing up into an adult dog with behavioural problems, and to avoid this you must ensure that your puppy has a wide range of good experiences with people, animals and things during the critical socialization period before he is twelve weeks old. Under-socialized dogs may become fearful, aggressive or destructive, and it is your responsibility as an owner to prevent this.

Meeting people

It is essential that your puppy encounters different people of all ages, appearances and personalities. So you should make a point of introducing him to children, teenagers, elderly friends and relatives, and people with beards or wearing uniforms. Your puppy will soon learn not to be fearful of strangers or to behave aggressively towards them.

You will have to wait until after his vaccinations to introduce your puppy to the people who visit your house regularly – the postman, the milkman and the refuse collectors. Let your friends and neighbours handle him and, when he is old enough, take him into town or to the park and let him mix with a wide range of people, although always on the lead and under your control.

Socialization with each other is very important for young puppies if they are to grow up into happy, well-adjusted adult dogs.

Household noises

A puppy should not be over-protected from household noises, and it is a good idea to get him accustomed from an early age to the sounds of a wide range of domestic appliances, including the vacuum cleaner, dishwasher, radio, television and washing machine. In addition, you could try exposing him to sudden loud noises; dropping a dustbin lid about 5m (15ft) away from him is not a bad idea.

Some dogs who can appear to be extremely confident with people and other animals are terrified of bangs, and therefore noisy thunderstorms and fireworks can be torture for them. Get your new puppy accustomed to noise from an early age.

Your puppy should meet as many new people as possible. You should encourage him to be both confident and friendly.

Puppy socialization classes are great fun and educational for the puppies and their owners. Your puppy will learn to interact with other dogs and people, and you can start some basic training.

Puppy socialization classes

These are sometimes a good way of getting your puppy accustomed to meeting other dog as well as a wide range of people. Ask your vet for the details of your nearest class; they are now widespread in most areas. He will not be able to go along until he has completed his course of vaccinations; indeed, many training and socialization classes will only accept puppies over 16 weeks of age. These classes are fun and very educational for both you and your puppy. As well as learning to mix and play with other dogs of different ages in a controlled environment, he will learn how to walk by your side on a lead without pulling and the basic obedience commands.

The experienced dog trainers will be able to advise you on caring for your puppy and can answer your questions on socialization and behaviour problems. If the class is run by your veterinary clinic, there may be qualified veterinary nurses on hand to whom you can talk about health issues.

Nervous puppies

It is essential that you socialize a fearful puppy or he may grow up into a nervous or aggressive adult. Protect him from aggressive older dogs and make sure that his experiences with other dogs are always enjoyable, playful ones. If you take him to a park or a public place, keep him on a lead – it can be a long, extending one – away from unfamiliar dogs. Handle him frequently, holding, stroking and grooming him. Take him out in the car with you to a wide range of places with different people and noises. Get him used to crowds, trains, buses and cyclists. It is also a good idea to make visiting the vet an enjoyable experience for him and to accustom him to being examined, having his mouth opened and nails clipped. This will make him a more confident dog.

must know

Problem behaviour
A properly socialized dog will rarely develop problem behaviour, so it is up to you to ensure that your puppy has a wide range of different enjoyable experiences. You could even create a range of controlled scenarios to introduce him to unfamiliar things and people, rewarding him when he reacts in a calm, confident way.

Puppies can learn about good manners and how to interact non-aggressively with other dogs by playing together.

Dangers and hazards

Your home can be a dangerous place for a puppy, so talk to your family about the hazards lurking inside the house and outside in the garden. A puppy will investigate everything he comes across, so don't leave any dangerous objects lying around.

Danger zones outside

Dogs like being outside and their garden becomes an extension of their territory. Puppies will explore every corner, so you must make your garden escape-proof; most puppies can squeeze through very small holes. As they grow, some of the taller breeds will jump 1–1.5m (3–5ft) if something attracts their attention. Securing wire netting on top of fencing and bending it over inwards towards the dog's territory will solve this particular problem. Make sure that all gates and garden doors close securely and cannot be opened by an inquisitive dog. Nor should there be a gap at the bottom under which he can crawl; if so, attach some strong wire netting at ground level.

Garden security

Take care when getting your car out – the puppy could be underneath. Get into the habit of checking up on him, always knowing where he is. Callers can leave gates open, so check they are closed before letting the puppy out into the garden. If you have a swimming pool or pond, it must be securely fenced. Other hazards within the garden include insecticides, poisons and slug bait – all poisonous to dogs. Even if you don't use these yourself, your neighbours might, so make sure that your garden is escape-proof.

Check also that there are no old cans of paint or varnish lying around, and that all the outside drains are properly covered. Puppies investigate everything they come across, so never think 'he won't touch that' because the odds are that he will. It is not easy to keep a new puppy off your cherished flower beds. The easiest way is to use very low wicker hurdles as temporary barriers. Puppies will delight in digging up what you have just planted and then proudly bringing their trophies to you. Spring bulbs are very dangerous, as are buttercups, azaleas, foxgloves and discarded foliage from privet and Leyland Cypress. Knowing what your puppy is doing and stopping him doing it is inevitably a relatively full-time occupation.

Almost everything in this garden shed poses some sort of danger to a dog. Never risk your dog having access to household or garden chemicals. It only takes a few seconds for him to lick a chemical or paint container or chew through an electric flex.

Danger zones inside

There are danger points for a young dog inside the
house, too. When they are young, long, low-slung
dogs, such as Basset Hounds and Dachshunds, as
well as large breeds, like Wolfhounds, should not be
allowed to go up and down stairs as their vertebrae
can become over-stressed, leading to spinal disc
troubles in later life. A child gate fitted at the bottom
of the stairs will put an effective stop to this activity.
If your puppy should accidentally climb the stairs,
always help him to come down safely, step by step.
A tumble downstairs at a young age could not only
injure him but also make him feel inhibited or fearful
about climbing any kind of steps later on in life.

Electrical hazards

Electrical sockets, plugs and trailing wires present
a range of interesting and chewable opportunities
for inquisitive puppies, so cover the wires, unplug
any appliances that are not in use and switch off
live sockets. You could even place a piece of furniture
in front of a socket. Be aware also that the on-off
switches on the hot-plates of a cooker can be
switched on easily by canine paws, so always turn
off the heat-source at the mains before you leave
the puppy loose in either the kitchen or utility room.

Be tidy

Train yourself to be tidy: hang tea cloths and towels
high up out of the puppy's reach. Children will have
to learn to live on a higher level. Their habit of leaving
their favourite toys lying around on the floor will be
tempting for the puppy who will pick up and chew
any small plastic ones. This can be very dangerous as

small pieces can lodge in a dog's stomach and even tear the lining, resulting in death or, at the very best, some expensive veterinary treatment.

Nor should you leave your favourite shoes at ground level – their scent will almost certainly prove irresistible to a teething pup. Puppies tend to mark their territory with urine, and any clothes and other objects left on the floor are seen as legitimate targets. Don't provide temptation and make sure you take the puppy outside regularly to prevent him soiling inside the house (see page 35).

Make cupboards dog-proof

Some clever puppies can open almost any door or cupboard. If this is a problem for you, attach some simple child-proof safety locks to them to prevent your dog gaining access. Do make sure that cleaning materials and chemicals are safely locked away and cannot be accessed by your dog.

Don't leave temptation in your puppy's way. Human food left where a puppy can easily reach it is usually far too irresistible.

Travelling with your puppy

Most dogs enjoy going out with their owners and like travelling in cars. It is a good idea to get your puppy accustomed to going in the car with you from the earliest possible age to prevent any negative associations with car travel in the future.

must know

Travel tips
When travelling with your puppy, no matter how short or long the journey, be sure to pack the following in the car:
• Towels for wiping muddy paws and drying off a wet dog
• A bottle of fresh water and a water bowl
• A collar and lead
• A blanket or 'vetbed' for the puppy to lie on
• A chewable toy or hide chew to keep him busy

Travel boxes or crates

These are beneficial for both the dog and car driver. If a dog is jumping around in your car, especially at high speeds, you will be distracted and cannot drive safely. A travel crate also offers security if you need to brake suddenly or your car is involved in an accident. If the doors were to fly open or the windows break, your dog could escape onto a busy road, becoming a danger to himself and traffic. It is easy to train your puppy to go into a crate by feeding him inside it; he will soon enter willingly and you can close the door for a short while to get him used to being inside.

When travelling, a puppy can be caged in a wire crate fitted with a small rug or blanket and some of his favourite toys.

Some owners of large dogs fit a dog guard or bars behind the passenger seats in a hatchback or estate car. However, if crates are introduced early in a dog's life, it has been shown that they help to reduce car sickness, nervous and hyperactive behaviour, as they induce a feeling of security in the dog and shield him from the visual stimuli that trigger the behaviour.

Acclimatizing your puppy

To get your puppy used to travelling by car, take him out for short journeys as frequently as possible. Drive slowly to avoid unnecessary motion, and take him to places with enjoyable associations, such as the park for a run or a friend's house for games.

Your dog will be safer travelling in a cage or special built-in crated area at the back of the car. Some have doors which can be locked.

Visiting the vet

Tell your vet that you are going to acquire a puppy and make sure he knows which breed you are contemplating, so he can find out in advance about any potential health problems before you take your new puppy along for his first check-up.

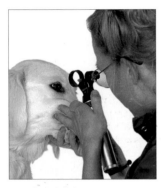

The vet will give your puppy a thorough examination and will look very closely at his eyes, ears, nose, mouth, paws and coat.

A pleasant experience

When the puppy has settled down, after a couple of days in his new home, you will need to take him to the veterinary clinic for his first set of vaccinations and to get him checked over by the vet. It is very important that this is a pleasant experience for the puppy to prevent him being anxious or aggressive when he goes to the clinic in later life. Regular handling and good socialization with a wide range of people will help to prepare him for the visit.

Do not put him down outside on the pavement between your home and the veterinary surgery or set him down on the floor of the surgery. Carry him at all times. Keep him well away from the inquisitive noses of other waiting dogs as there is a risk of infection, and most dogs visiting the veterinary surgery are there because there is something wrong with them.

Vaccinations

The vet will give your puppy a general examination and will vaccinate him. Several canine diseases are a threat to your dog's life, especially parvovirus, distemper and leptospirosis, and it is essential that he is inoculated against these. Most vets will perform the initial vaccination between 10 and 12 weeks, with the booster following two weeks later. If the puppy is deemed to be not old enough for vaccinations, then do make an appointment at the first opportunity.

Puppies should not go out in a public place until about 10 days after the course of vaccinations is complete. Your vet will be able to advise you whether there are any potentially dangerous places locally. Never make the mistake of stopping in a roadside lay-by for your puppy to go the toilet, as these places are hotbeds of infection.

Insurance

Ask the vet anything that might be bothering you about your puppy's diet, behaviour or health and also about taking out pet insurance. Puppies are vulnerable to disease and it is always a wise move to take out insurance because of the ever-escalating costs of veterinary services. Several reputable companies specialize in this area, offering different levels of cover, so ask your vet for advice.

When you take your puppy for his first vaccination, the vet will check him all over to assess his general state of health.

Play and games

A puppy needs to be stimulated with lots of things to do. In the wild, he would be taught to track animals, fight predators and catch prey, but pet dogs don't need these skills and it's up to you to provide exciting alternatives in the form of play and games.

must know

Energetic breeds
Some working breeds, such as Collies and Springer Spaniels, have boundless energy and need a lot of mental stimulation as well as exercise to prevent them becoming bored and destructive and developing behavioural problems as adults. Do not consider owning such a dog unless you can commit to spending a lot of time together and enjoy long walks.

Games you can play

Puppies tend to be very lively and they need physical and mental exercise if they are to grow up into fit, healthy, well-behaved dogs. Playing games together can use up excess energy and create a bond between you and your puppy. First of all, you will have to teach him how to play safely with you and toys, without grabbing, biting or being destructive.

Most games for dogs invariably involve catching, retrieving and playing hide-and-seek. Dogs derive the most fun out of chasing and retrieving balls. Start when your puppy is young by throwing a ball just in front of him, and then make a fuss of him when he returns it and persuade him gently to 'drop' it rather than running off with it. Praise and reward him when he gives it to you, and then throw it again. He will soon realize that it is worth his while to come back and relinquish the object, When he is proficient at retrieving, hide the ball for him to find – close by initially but gradually increasing the distance.

Some dogs adore pushing a football with their nose, and your children can have fun playing footie with their pet. Quoit rings are fun to throw and pull, but the ultimate throwing game is with a 'Frisbee'. Dogs get great exercise running after it and leaping into the air to catch it.

Your puppy will enjoy playing games and you should provide him with a range of interesting toys to keep him occupied. Make time each day to play with him.

Suitable toys

By playing with your puppy, you will minimize the chances of him becoming bored and then engaging in destructive behaviour. Most dog toys are now virtually indestructible, although not totally, as you will soon find out. Many dogs, particularly Terriers, adore squeaky toys and will not be content until they have found the squeak and 'killed' it. Sometimes, however, they may adopt a soft toy, which Retrievers or Spaniels will carry about in their mouth.

Do not play tug-of-war, even with a soft toy – you will be training your puppy to be destructive and possessive as well as encouraging him to use his strength against you. This could be counter-productive if he grows up into a large, powerful dog. All dogs can be taught to play with a ball but do be careful that

Puppies enjoy playing with tug toys and chews. Squeaky toys are less suitable for Terriers who will destroy them while searching for the squeaking device!

Toys

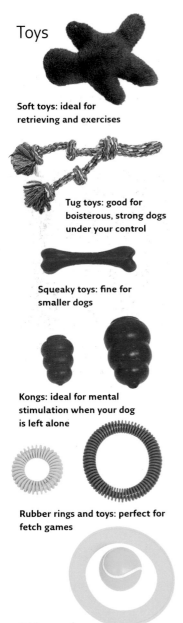

Soft toys: ideal for retrieving and exercises

Tug toys: good for boisterous, strong dogs under your control

Squeaky toys: fine for smaller dogs

Kongs: ideal for mental stimulation when your dog is left alone

Rubber rings and toys: perfect for fetch games

Frisbees and tennis balls: ideal for playing outdoor games of fetch

the ball is not too small. Dogs' jaws can open very wide and they can swallow quite large objects. If they should accidentally swallow a rubber or plastic ball the repercussions could be serious. Nor should you give your puppy an old shoe or slipper to chew and destroy – dogs notoriously ignore the difference between old and new shoes.

Good pet shops stock a variety of suitable toys, and you should choose ones that claim to be indestructible with no metal or plastic. The 'Kong' is particularly good and much loved by dogs. This hollow, strangely shaped thick rubber ball can be stuffed with small food titbits. Your dog will chase it happily for hours, trying to get the food out. Alternatively, if you are going out for a while and leaving your puppy shut up in the house, a Kong will amuse him. He can chew it or move it around the floor to release the hidden treats it contains. Nylon bones will also keep dogs occupied as well as cleaning their teeth.

Good manners

Games and playing with toys provide opportunities for teaching your puppy good manners. He will soon learn that it is not acceptable to be over-boisterous and to jump up or grab your arm or hand to get a toy. He has to take care not to bite you and if he does so, even by accident in play, you must remove the toy and stop the game immediately. He must also learn how to let go of a toy when asked to do so. Always take it away from underneath his head so that he cannot see what you are planning to do. Grasp the toy tightly and tell him to 'drop' it while offering him a tasty treat. If he is motivated by food, he should drop the toy to take the treat.

Exercise

Young puppies can get all the exercise they need from their own exuberance when running about and playing, and there is no need for any formal exercise. In fact, it could harm their development if they are forced into too much activity at too young an age.

When to start exercising

The age varies from breed to breed, but between five and six months is usual – the breeder or your vet can advise. For large dogs, such as Irish Wolfhounds, too much exercise can be harmful for a puppy whose bones are still growing. However, it is a good idea to take even a young puppy for short walks on a lead.

Most puppies will enjoy playing 'fetch' with a ball. It allows them to run freely and have some fun.

Lead training

Begin lead training as soon as the puppy arrives. Get him used to wearing a collar, then add a light lead; he will quickly get accustomed to it trailing after him. Pick up the lead and follow him without applying any pressure. After a while, assert some light pressure and gently guide him. Talk to him all the time in an encouraging way to boost his confidence. Make sure the collar is sufficiently tight that he cannot slip out of it, but not so tight that it is strangling him. Continue these sessions outside in the garden. Make it fun and train in short bursts as puppies become easily bored.

When your puppy is ready to go out for a proper walk, remember that noisy traffic can be frightening, so carry him around the block two or three times for a day or two before you put him down. Speak to him gently all the while to build up his confidence – he knows you are there to protect him.

Your social responsibilities

Behavioural scientists have now proved that owning a dog is beneficial to adults and children, but in the light of today's social attitudes you must train your dog to fit into modern society's perception of what constitutes acceptable social behaviour.

Aggressive dogs

The 1991 UK Dangerous Dogs Act gave the courts new powers to deal with dogs that were perceived to be dangerous. As a dog owner, you should be aware of your responsibilities and take steps to prevent your dog behaving aggressively. Socialization helps your puppy to grow up into a

It is natural for a dog to bark as a warning to people approaching his territory, but he must not bark excessively or your neighbours may complain.

confident, friendly dog who can accompany you in public. If he does show signs of aggression, keep him on a lead, fit a muzzle if needed and seek help from a pet behaviour counsellor.

Fouling public places

Many local authorities have introduced dog 'no-go' areas, especially on beaches and in parks, and are enforcing 'dog fouling' by-laws under which owners can be fined if they allow their dog to foul public places without picking up the mess. There are many ways of doing this and various gadgets are sold to pick up dog faeces. You would be wise to always carry something to scoop up dog mess, even if it's just a plastic bag, when you're out walking your dog.

want to know more?

• For more detailed information on owning a puppy, read *Collins Puppy Handbook* by Gwen Bailey.

weblinks

• For practical advice on puppy care go to the Blue Cross website at www.bluecross.org.uk
• To buy specialist puppy equipment online, see www.petplanet.co.uk
• To find a vet in your area, look at www.rcvs.org.uk
• For puppy training classes, visit the website of the Association of Pet Dog Trainers at www.apdt.co.uk

Always pick up your dog's mess and use your walks to help him develop social skills.

3 The adult dog

At around 18 months, your puppy will develop
into a mature adult. You will still have to care
for him on a daily basis. Not only will you have
to feed, exercise and groom him but also play
games together and arrange for him to be well
looked after if you go away on holiday. If you
know how to keep your dog fit and healthy,
mentally and physically, you can prevent many
common health and behavioural problems. In
this section, you will find expert practical advice
on every aspect of looking after your adult dog.

Feeding an adult dog

Food, walks and play are the highlights of your dog's day. As he has no control over what he is given to eat, as an owner you should give him the most nutritious food that you can afford.

Why diet is important

Canines are among the most remarkable of animals as far as food is concerned: they can live on the most unlikely foodstuffs or, rather, they can subsist on them, but incorrect or bad feeding will inevitably result in health problems, such as skin disorders, hysteria, obesity, muscle wasting and shortening of life.

Food requirements are different for every breed and for individual dogs within a breed. They are based on size and energy output, so a hound or a gundog working in the field needs more food, calories and protein than a sedentary dog of the same breed.

Types of dog food

A bewildering array of dog food is available, each one claiming to be the ultimate nutritious food for your pet. However, for the novice dog owner, it is probably advisable to be guided by your vet or dog breeder.

Complete dry food

This is one of the most popular convenience foods for dogs. It is mostly composed of cereals and their by-products, meat from various sources, vegetables, soya, oils, fats, vitamins and minerals, but there may be colourants and preservatives, too. Dry foods can be marketed in many forms, such as biscuits, pellets, meal or extruded products. They are easy to store.

Semi-moist foods

These foods contain up to 25 per cent moisture and, to avoid refrigeration, some preservatives. Their composition is similar to that of other commercial dog foods and they are easy to feed and to store.

Canned foods

These are often more than 75 per cent moisture but the best ones are nutritionally complete with similar ingredients to other dog foods. Unless otherwise stated, most of these foods do contain preservatives and colourings which may make them unsuitable for dogs with allergies or skin problems.

Canned food is mainly made up of meat, offal and tripe, augmented by vitamins and minerals. This food is usually served with extruded pellets which are better known as 'mixers' and come in different sizes, flavours and compositions.

Feeding your dog

The argument as to whether it's better to feed your dog once or twice a day has still not been resolved. Modern thinking dictates that if a dog has food in his stomach he is more likely to be calm and content, so it is preferable to feed him twice a day. This gives him two high points in his day. Most people who follow this regime divide the food into three parts, one of which is given in the morning and two in the evening. However, it is more convenient for some people to feed their dog one main meal a day, usually in the evening. They argue that this system reduces the risk of over-feeding and obesity. Whichever system you adopt and whatever type of food you serve, unlimited fresh water must be available at all times.

must know

Obesity
Thirty per cent of pet dogs are overweight and need special attention, as extra weight can reduce their life span. If your dog is obese, ask your vet to recommend a special diet and proper exercise. Do not give a dog of any age sweet biscuits, candy and cakes. Chocolate is also banned as it is high in fat and sugar, can be toxic to some dogs or cause circulatory problems, particularly in small breeds. Use specially formulated dog treats or small pieces of cooked liver as food rewards.

Food guarding

Your dog should not snap or growl at you or other pets when he is eating. It is important that he feels safe when he is fed and knows that the food will not be taken away from him before he finishes it. This process starts in puppyhood when dogs learn that human hands provide goodies rather than taking them away. If your dog does guard his food aggressively, you may need to seek professional help to solve the problem.

Fresh food

Some people prefer to prepare and cook their dog's food themselves. Meat can be served either raw or lightly cooked and accompanied by some vegetables, rice or even pasta. The amounts fed will vary but, as a general guide, a 10kg (22lb) dog should have 300g (10oz) of meat, 75g (3oz) of rice and a similar amount of vegetables. Although undoubtedly tasty and healthy, the problem with feeding fresh food is that there may be a deficiency of some minerals and vitamins, so you may have to add a high-quality supplement. Ask your vet for advice on this as over-supplementation may cause health problems.

Table scraps are not usually suitable food for dogs, although there is no reason why left-over meat and vegetables should not be added to your dog's food provided that they do not exceed the normal portion.

How much food?

Most dogs will eat everything that is placed in front of them but they should not be allowed to put on excessive weight. Ideally, a smooth-haired dog's ribs should be just visible, and his calorific input (food) should not exceed his output (exercise). Commercially prepared foods recommend approximate amounts for different breeds, sizes and ages, so read the labels. However, do bear in mind that every dog is different.

Chews and bones

Dogs love gnawing on hide chews and raw marrow bones. Never give cooked bones, especially chicken and game bones, as they can splinter and the dog could choke. Be careful about offering bones if your dog is possessive and make him behave aggressively.

Opposite: Make sure that your dog is fed nutritious meals which supply all the essential nutrients he needs for good health.

Exercise and play

Most dogs look forward to going out for walks on the lead or for a run in the local countryside or park. They need both free running and lead-walking for their physical and mental well-being.

How much exercise?

Your dog will need to be exercised, either on a lead or running free, every day, but the amount needed will depend on his size, conformation, breed and age. Most dogs can take as much exercise as their owner can give, but if you live in a built-up area then two good walks a day and a run at the weekend are the minimum that you should give your dog. You can also exercise your dog in the garden: just 30 minutes' playing with a ball or Frisbee is good exercise for him.

All dogs need daily exercise. As well as walking on a lead, it is a good idea to give your dog a period of free running if possible.

Hounds, gundogs, working and pastoral dogs

These dogs generally require a great deal of exercise, and you must be prepared to walk them several miles a day. They are designed to move over great distances, and thus a stroll round the block twice a day is unlikely to keep them in optimum condition. They are suited to country living where there is space for them to run. Gundogs will also enjoy swimming and it may be hard to keep them out of ponds and rivers. You must realize that dogs kept alone do not have the motivation for running about unless they hunt, and it is up to you to provide the motivation.

Terriers, utility and toy dogs

Dogs from the Terrier group and also some from the utility and toy groups are busy and energetic. They like exploring gardens, sniffing about in bushes and long grass, play-hunting, looking for mice or rats and trying to catch birds. They also enjoy going for walks, seeing new things and smelling new scents.

A regular walk twice a day and a long run in your local fields or woods will be beneficial for both of you. These types of dogs are usually very playful right up into old age – an hour spent with the children in the garden playing 'catch' or 'hide and seek' in addition to their routine walks occupies their mind and keeps them out of mischief, especially Terrier breeds.

Toy breeds, such as Pekingeses, Chihuahuas, Pugs and Pomeranians, will need very little in the way of formal exercise – just a short walk round the block on a lead or their normal activities plus some playing in the garden are usually sufficient. However, they love to go out on excursions with their owners, even if it means carrying them.

Grooming

There are several very good reasons why you should groom your dog regularly. The act of gentle grooming – the passage of a comb pulled through the hair and the brushing – gives a pleasurable feeling to the dog and it assists in the bonding process.

Why grooming is important

Regular grooming gives you the ideal opportunity to examine your pet – to look for any skin conditions, cuts, abrasions, discharges or parasites. You can prevent many common health problems developing by looking for the early tell-tale signs. Some breeds, especially long-haired ones, require a daily grooming session, whereas others with shorter coats need only weekly attention. Smooth-coated dogs will require a

A longer-haired dog, such as this Golden Retriever, will require regular grooming to keep his coat in good condition and remove any mats, tangles and dead hairs.

twice-weekly brush and polish. Regular grooming, particularly when dogs are moulting, will prevent their cast-off hairs covering carpets and furniture.

Some coats tangle and matt very easily. They are uncomfortable for the dog and a hot bed of infection, an ideal place for bugs to breed. Some moulting dogs experience matting and thus it is important that you gently tease out and remove the dead hair.

Grooming is not difficult, and even the advanced preparation needed for showing a dog can be learnt by anyone. The breed clubs have grooming charts and will give you advice, and most breed books have chapters on show preparation and the tools required.

When to start grooming

You should start grooming your puppy from the earliest possible age, especially if he has a long coat that will require a lot of attention later on. Grooming should be a pleasurable experience for both of you, so keep the sessions short initially to prevent the dog becoming restless. You can extend them gradually as he grows older and more accustomed to them.

Grooming equipment

The amount of grooming equipment you require will depend on your dog's coat type. If you own a Pug, for example, all you need is a brush and comb, but if you have a Poodle you must invest in some hairdresser's scissors, electric clippers and several blades, a hair dryer, and a set of specialist brushes and combs.

Owners of dogs with wire coats will need stripping knives of various types and sizes plus special palm brushes with very short teeth and maybe even a rake for controlling the dog's undercoat.

Tools of the trade

Wide- and fine-toothed combs

Soft pin brush

Bristle brush

Stripping comb

Thinning scissors

Pointed-end scissors

Nail clippers

Brush

Coat types

Strictly speaking, there are as many coat types as there are dog breeds and there are different types within breeds. The first division is into three types: short-haired (Dobermann), medium-length (German Shepherd Dog) and long-haired (Yorkshire Terrier). These divisions can be sub-divided into smooth, rough, wiry and curly. A further division is soft, medium and harsh. Different coat types demand special grooming tools, treatment and handling. However, with a few exceptions, they all have an undercoat of various textures, thicknesses and colours.

Whereas some dogs are born with the colour that stays all their life, others change. Kerry Blue Terriers start black and finish blue/grey. Yorkshire Terriers start black and tan and finish blue/grey and golden tan. Puppy hair is fluffy and bears no relationship to adult hair – although it can be removed, it is best to wait for it to drop out naturally with brushing.

If you own a Dobermann with its distinctive glossy, short-haired coat, grooming will be minimal.

Short-haired dogs

The hair on short-haired dogs is invariably smooth and relatively thin and it usually has a very fine undercoat. It is the easiest coat to care for, needing only an occasional brush to remove any dead hairs, and a polish with a hound glove or a chamois leather to distribute the coat oils and give it a shine.

Although these short coats appear to be silky to the touch, a closer examination will show that the hair is really quite harsh. The fact that it lies flat and close gives the impression of silkiness, but stroke it in the opposite direction to the way in which it lies and it is quite spiky. The short coat of a Bullmastiff is said to be hard. The coat of the Shar Pei is described as short and bristly. Most of these short coats are self cleaning – they do not absorb water and when they dry any mud or dirt will just fall off.

Medium-haired dogs

Dogs with medium-length coats will require more grooming than most short-haired dogs but less than long-haired breeds. Most dogs in this category will only need brushing and combing two or three times a week to keep their coats in good condition and to remove mud and tangles. The smooth-coated Collie has a medium-length smooth coat which, although dense, is harsh to the touch – it is waterproof by virtue of the thick undercoat.

Medium-haired dogs need a daily grooming session but not too long.

Long-haired dogs

Long coats are some of the most time-consuming ones to keep in good condition. The softer they are, the more they are likely to tangle and the more dirt and debris they will pick up. It is not really feasible to keep a long-haired dog in full coat as an ordinary pet. The flowing white coat of the Maltese, the distinctive, silky floor-length coat of the Yorkshire Terrier or the sweeping locks of the Shih Tzu present countless difficulties for the pet owner. If you intend to show your dog, you will be prepared to put in the time and effort needed to groom these dogs properly.

Most pet owners keep their long-haired dogs in a short cut, known in some breeds as a 'puppy cut'. It is relatively simple to train the dog to stand on a table and, using a pair of sharp scissors, to give him the rough shape of the breed. Dogs prefer to have short hair than to have knotted long coats. Once a year, perhaps, they can go to a professional

An adult Yorkshire Terrier has a silky long-haired coat which will need regular grooming, even if you don't show your pet.

This Jack Russell Terrier has a rough, water-resistant coat which is typical of many Terriers.

Rough Collies have a long, thick coat which needs a lot of time and attention to keep it healthy.

groomer to be shaped properly. Old English Sheepdogs are difficult to maintain and the coats matt very easily. Therefore they are often taken to the grooming parlour to have all their hair shorn off in the manner of a sheep, especially if they live in the country and run free.

Rough-haired dogs

This type of coat consists of harsh, stand-off outer guard hairs and a soft undercoat, whose thickness will vary according to the breed. Spitz-type dogs, such as the Chow Chow, have a very thick undercoat whereas Rough Collies have much less but their outer coat is longer and more luxurious. All these breeds moult copious amounts of hair which, if left, can get knotted and cause irritation, so they need regular grooming. Dirt and dust tend to gather in the undercoat, which should be deep combed. The area surrounding the anus can become very unhygienic while male dogs' coats can be stained with urine underneath, so pay special attention to these areas.

Poodles

Poodles do not moult, but if their hair was left to grow it would eventually become corded or felted. Most people keep their Poodles in a 'puppy cut' whereby the coat is scissored all over to a length of about 5cm (2in) with the face, feet and rear trimmed close to the skin. With practice, most owners can manage this but those who cannot should take their dog to the grooming parlour once every eight weeks. The dog should be brushed and combed every day.

Wire-haired breeds

These breeds need special attention. If the hair is cut, it tends to lose its texture and the colour will gradually fade. The proper treatment for this type of coat is to hand-strip or pluck it. This is an art that can only be achieved with practice and an understanding of the coat growth. For example, the hair on the body of a Welsh Terrier should be just over 2.5cm (1in) in length, the neck hair thicker, the head hair very short, and the furnishings on the legs profuse.

To keep a Poodle's coat in good condition, you will either have to trim him regularly yourself or visit the grooming parlour.

To achieve this sort of result, stand the dog on a table. Hold the skin where the hair is to be removed with one hand and, with a stripping knife in the other hand, trap a few of the longest hairs between your thumb and the stripping knife. Pull the hairs out evenly and smoothly without jerking. Slowly, over several weeks, the required shape will appear. Most owners, however, do not go to all this trouble; instead, they take their dog to a grooming parlour once every three months and they clip it into shape.

You can hand-strip a dog any time by pulling out a few hairs between your forefinger and thumb. Do it when you are sitting down together in the evening.

It is easy to hand-strip a Terrier. Just take a few hairs between your thumb and forefinger and pull gently. It won't hurt your dog.

Grooming techniques

Try to make grooming your dog a pleasurable experience for both of you. If you develop a grooming routine while your dog is still a puppy, he will soon come to accept and enjoy this time you spend together. Depending on the breed, you can groom him on your lap, down on the floor or up on a table.

Brushing your dog

The type of brush you use will depend on his coat type. Always be gentle and do not hurt your dog. To remove really matted tangles, it is sometimes a good idea to tease them out with your fingers before gently pulling a brush or comb through them. If they are very bad indeed, you may even have to cut them out carefully with sharp scissors.

Brushing long ears

Dogs with long ears should have them brushed every day and also checked for tangles and foreign objects, especially after a walk. Begin by teasing out any thick tangles at the end of the ear flap with your fingers. Then start at the top of the ears, slowly but smoothly brushing down to the ends. Placing a hand under the ear flap at the base of the ear will prevent pulling on the sensitive skin around the ear opening. Excess hair is always best plucked out with your fingers as scissoring may allow hairs to fall into the ear.

Grooming tails and rear ends

There are many different styles of dogs' tails, most of which do not require much attention. Very hairy hanging tails probably need the most grooming. Carefully cut the hair away from where it touches

must know

Stripping knives

These are often used on breeds such as Spaniels. It is best to watch a professional at work before attempting it yourself on your dog. If you are interested in stripping your dog, find out about grooming classes in your area. Many breed societies run them.

the dog's anus with sharp scissors, preferably those with a slight curve. Otherwise give the area a routine brush and comb. Keep the folds of skin clean on very short tails, such as the Bulldog's. Wire-haired breeds should have the underside of the tail kept short.

Nearly every medium- and long-haired dog needs to have his or her rear end kept clear of excessive hair for obvious reasons. Take great care as the area is very delicate; curved scissors prevent accidental 'digging in'. Bitches can suffer staining of the hair on the hind legs, which is known as 'culottes'. Excessive hair growth on the male's penis sheath should be cut very carefully for hygiene purposes.

Using a slicker

To groom short-haired hounds and Terriers, you will need to use a tool called a slicker or hound glove. Made of rubber, it glides easily through the dog's coat and massages the skin underneath.

Bathing
It is rarely necessary to bathe gundogs, Hounds or Terriers. If they get muddy, wait for them to dry and then brush them. Don't bath your dog too often as it removes the natural oils in his coat. Sit a small dog in a bowl or sink and wash with tepid water. Use a bath for larger dogs. Lather the coat with a dog shampoo, protecting the eyes and ears, then rinse thoroughly. Gently towel dry and then use a hair dryer if the dog will accept it. Don't let him lie in a draught or cool place until he is dry.

One way to dry a dog is to put him in a zip-up towelling bag after towel-drying him. This will keep him snug and warm until he is thoroughly dry all over.

Examining your dog

Any dog who comes from a caring breeder should, with regular healthcare, lead a long and healthy vet-free life. You can prevent many common health disorders occurring, or nip them in the bud, by examining your dog on a regular basis.

must know

Soft-mouthed dogs
If you own a dog with a soft mouth, such as a Spaniel, check the folds of skin around his mouth frequently for any food residues. If left, these can lead to bad breath, gum disease and other dental problems.

When to do it

A good time to examine your dog is during a regular grooming session. Look especially at the eyes, ears, mouth and genital area for any unusual discharges. If you notice something out of the ordinary, consult your vet. After country walks, examine your dog's feet and body for cuts, abrasions, ticks and fleas.

Dental care

A puppy's baby teeth will fall out during the first few months but in some toy breeds the baby teeth will persist and the second teeth will not dislodge them. If this happens, veterinary treatment is necessary to remove the first teeth and allow sufficient room for the adult teeth to come through. Like humans, all dogs produce tartar and plaque, which may be due to our modern feeding regimes. If these substances are allowed to build up, they will trap pockets of bacteria which can cause gum disease, rotting teeth and bad breath. It may even become necessary for your vet to remove the deposits under a general anaesthetic.

Cleaning your dog's teeth
You can avoid many of these problems by brushing your dog's teeth. If you start when he is young, it is relatively easy to train him to have his teeth cleaned;

it just needs patience and kindness at the beginning. You can buy specially formulated toothpastes for dogs as well as brushes which are designed for their mouths. Never use your own human toothpaste, which is designed specifically for our use; dogs find these toothpastes offensive.

Chewing

Hard biscuits are good for a dog's teeth, as are chews that are specifically designed for cleaning teeth. Many of these can be purchased in supermarkets, pet shops or veterinary clinics. Chewing on a bone is a classic remedy but only give your dog big raw marrow bones – never cooked chicken or lamb bones or any little bones that can splinter and pierce the stomach lining, causing death. If you do give your dog bones, you must teach him to give them up to you when he is requested to do so, or he may become possessive and aggressive.

Chewing on chews, hard biscuits and bones will help to clean a dog's teeth, so that they stay strong and healthy.

Caring for eyes

The eyes of some dog breeds, such as Pugs, protrude slightly and are set forward in the skull. This makes them very vulnerable to scratches from playing in the bushes and running through the undergrowth. When grooming your dog, examine him carefully for any marks on the eyes themselves. Check if there is excess tear staining in the surrounding fur or deposits in the corner of the eyes. If there is any evidence of scratches, ulcers or infection, such as conjunctivitis, contact the vet immediately. Even if there is no evidence of injury, there may be particles of dust in the eye. If so, bathe gently with some cotton wool soaked in Optrex. You can remove tear staining from a white coat with special products available from pet shops.

Feet and claws

Check your dog's feet regularly, trimming back the hair if necessary. Leave some between the pads but keep it clean. Tease out any tangles with your fingers. Grass seeds can embed themselves into the pad and migrate up a dog's leg so always check for these in the summer months.

Claws should be kept short. However, great care should be taken when cutting claws as there is a sensitive part containing a vein and to cut into this causes great pain and an outpouring of blood. Before undertaking this task yourself, watch an expert or the vet and ask them to show you how to trim them.

Should your dog develop a limp when out walking, examine his feet carefully for any damage. If there is a deep cut, you should apply pressure bandages immediately. Any significant cut should receive urgent veterinary treatment.

must know

Protuberant eyes
Some dogs, such as Pugs and Pekingeses, have slightly bulging eyes, and you must check them regularly for any signs of ulceration or infection. The folds in their face and the crease above their nose will need daily cleaning with some damp cotton wool. If they become very dry, smear them with a little petroleum jelly.

Ear hygiene

Some breeds are more prone to ear infections than others, and dogs with erect ears tend to suffer less than those with floppy ears, the reason being that erect ears allow the circulation of air. Floppy ears trap warm, moist air, creating an ideal breeding place for bugs. The first indication of an ear infection is when the dog persistently shakes his head and scratches an ear deeply and slowly. When this happens, it is almost certain that you are already too late to apply home remedies and a visit to the vet is indicated.

The vet will probably prescribe some ear drops which should clear up the ear infection relatively quickly. However, failure to do so will certainly result in a dog becoming so irritated by the condition that his general health will deteriorate.

You can clean your dog's ears with a specially formulated cleanser. Just aim the nozzle of the container into the ear canal and then squeeze very gently.

Keeping your dog's ears clean

You can keep your dog's ears clean and healthy by wiping them once a week with a specially formulated ear cleansing liquid which is available from most pet shops or your veterinary clinic. It is simple to use: all you need do is squeeze a little into the ear and then wipe clean with some cotton wool or tissue. If your dog objects to this, wrap him firmly within a towel while you do it or ask someone to hold him for you.

The excess hair inside the ears of some breeds can harbour mites and therefore it should be plucked out with your fingers. Do not cut it with scissors or the hairs will fall into the dog's ear. Long ears should always be cleaned and combed after exercise as they may become matted and muddy. To feed these dogs, always use a tall, narrow dish so that their ears stay free and clean and are not immersed in the food.

Massage the ear gently with your hand. If wished, use some cotton wool soaked in cleanser to clean the accessible parts of the ear.

Travelling and holidays

If you are planning to go away on holiday, with or without your dog, you must make the appropriate arrangements for his welfare. Luckily, it is now possible to stay in many dog-friendly hotels, B-and-Bs, and self-catering holiday cottages and apartments.

must know

Elderly dogs
Unless an old dog is full of vigour don't take him on long journeys. It's no problem if he is used to boarding kennels. If not, leave him with a trusted friend whom he knows and who will feed and exercise him in the way he understands. You can also use a dog sitter who will stay in your home and look after the dog. Don't rely on neighbours popping in to feed and exercise him – he is not their dog and they can too easily forget.

What's best for the dog?

There is no reason why a pet dog should ever be left at home; he can either be taken on holiday with you or left in the care of a reputable boarding kennel, house sitter or friend. Many hotels and guest houses in the UK will accept dogs, so you could consider taking your dog with you. You can obtain a list of suitable accommodation from the local tourist information office, which can also advise on whether dogs are prohibited on their beaches at certain times of the year. However, there is often a deserted stretch of sand away from the fashionable beaches where a dog can run and swim as he pleases.

Travelling

Buses and coaches only accept dogs at the driver's or conductor's discretion. If the dog occupies a seat, a fee may be charged. Dogs usually travel on trains free of charge provided they are under control and do not occupy a seat. When flying in Britain and some European countries, dogs are not permitted to travel in the cabin with you; they have to travel in appropriate-sized boxes in the hold and you are charged a high fee for the privilege. Details are available from individual airlines or from agents who specialize in the transport of live animals.

When travelling by car, it is best to put your dog in a travelling crate, which is safer for both of you. Get him used to the crate by feeding him inside it with the door open. After a day or so, close the door. He will soon accept it and will enjoy being in his own box. Go through the same procedure in the car and then drive slowly for a short distance every day for a week. Go somewhere the dog connects with pleasure – the park, beach or some open ground where he can run. If the dog is travel sick after this training, consult the vet, but do not use human remedies.

Feeding your dog

Do not change your dog's food when on holiday; he may suffer an upset stomach. If ordinary and easily available complete diet or canned food is the norm, there is no need to take food with you. If he needs special food – for instance, he may be elderly with a kidney dysfunction – you would be wise to pack the right food. For a day out, there are food carriers that are specially designed to hold a day's food and water, keeping them hygienic and cool.

Hot days

All dogs suffer badly from heat, especially thick-coated, short-nosed and black ones, so on hot days take ice packs or bags of frozen peas to place on the heads of overheated dogs. Never leave your dog in a car in the sun; even with the windows open, he can be 'cooked' to death in a short time. If a dog shows heat distress, his tongue will loll fully out, he will pant deeply and be unwilling to move. Pack him with ice, immerse him fully in cold water and then get him to a vet as a matter of urgency. Always carry water in hot weather.

Never leave your dog in a car on a hot day. Even out in the open air, many dogs, especially ones with thick coats, may not be able to stay cool. With his lolling tongue, heavy panting and tired appearance, this dog is showing the classic signs of heat distress.

Pet Travel Scheme

It is now possible for dog owners to take their pets
on holiday with them within the European Union
and some other designated rabies-free countries.
However, there are some stringent rules that must
be followed before you can take your dog abroad. If
you are planning an overseas holiday with your dog
or own a house in Europe and want to travel back
and forth regularly with your pet, talk to your vet
about what must be done at least six months before
you plan to go away. It is a complex and relatively
expensive process as outlined below:

- A microchip must be inserted in the dog.
- The dog must be vaccinated against rabies.
- The dog must be blood tested 30 days after the
vaccination.
- You must have a DEFRA re-entry certificate that
confirms the above six months after the blood test
gives positive results.
- Between 24 and 48 hours before your return to
the UK, the dog must be treated by a vet against ticks
and other parasites and have a veterinary certificate
to prove this.
- You must sign a document to the effect that the
dog has not left the qualifying countries.

Everything must be in order on your return home;
if not, your dog will have to go into quarantine. These
regulations are subject to change, so check them out
before leaving the UK and re-entering the country.
You must obey any local regulations that apply in the
countries you are passing through and the country
in which you are staying. For instance, if you stay in
France for more than one month, your dog will have
to be tattooed according to the French law.

The nearest DEFRA office will advise on the exact requirements as far as British and foreign regulations are concerned. Your vet should know about any unusual diseases your dog may come into contact with and the steps you can take to avoid them. For the latest information, visit the DEFRA website.

Travelling tips

Take your dog's usual food with you and break the journey regularly so he can relieve himself. Keep a bottle of water and a bowl in the car. Dogs are often better received in Europe than in Britain but not all hotels accept them, so check in advance. One of the pleasures of travelling abroad is how many cafés and restaurants welcome dogs. They can sit by your feet under the table or even be served a drink or meal.

want to know more?

• For information on the Pet Travel Scheme, look at the DEFRA website: www.defra.gov.uk
• Collins have a wide range of petcare books for dog owners. Look on their website at www.collins.co.uk

weblinks

• For a range of organic and natural foods for dogs, go to www.petorganic.com
• The Blue Cross website advises on many aspects of dog ownership with practical advice and support for new owners: www.bluecross.org.uk

Many dogs enjoy car travel and they will happily accompany their owners when they go on holiday.

4 Training your dog

A well-behaved dog is a pleasure to own and will become a much-loved member of your family. Training need not be a tedious chore. It can be enjoyable and beneficial for both you and your dog if it is approached in the right frame of mind. You need to be patient and work together as a team. It's important to make your dog understand what it is you want him to do and reward him when he does it. If you keep the sessions short, repeat them frequently and use reward-based methods, your dog will soon learn to obey your commands and will enjoy pleasing you.

Make training fun

You can make training fun. Like any kind of education, whether it is designed for children or puppies, sometimes the going is tough and you or your dog may despair of ever getting it right, but the joy of having a well-mannered, happy dog who is a credit to you in any situation makes all the hard work worthwhile.

must know

Useful commands
Here are some useful commands that you should use with your dog. You cannot teach your puppy all these words immediately. Introduce them slowly and he will soon learn to respond to them in the correct way:
- 'Sit'
- 'Stay'
- 'Come'
- 'Down'
- 'Fetch'
- 'Drop'
- 'Bed'
- 'Hi five'
- 'Find'

Benefits of training

The well-trained dog is a happy dog. He rarely gets into trouble because he has behaved badly without being aware that he is doing so. He is seldom if ever shut away because he is a nuisance. The dog who has been trained to be a tolerable member of our society flourishes in the approval of his owner, his family and their circle of friends.

The well-trained dog is unable to reason that because he is well-trained he is able to go on a lot more outings than a badly-behaved dog, but this is the case. If you can trust your dog to behave well, he can accompany you to the countryside, the park and interesting beaches. He can walk through woodland and visit all the places where other dogs can be encountered and enjoyed.

The trained dog has a wider social life, and so will you! If both you and your family take a pleasure in obedience training you may decide to take the skill to further lengths – for instance, you may want to join a local class for more advanced training or even proceed to competition level with your dog. But first of all, you and your puppy must master the initial kindergarten stage of training and learn to execute the basic commands.

Get a language

Before you bring your new puppy home, draw up a short list of the words that you will use to train him. Make the words as simple as possible, easy to say, and distinctive from one another.

You may want to make your word for 'go and pass urine or defecate in the garden or on the patio' a secret code word, so that you can use it anywhere in public without any embarrassment. The Guide Dogs for the Blind Association use 'Hurry up!' – as good a praise as any for the purpose. However, remember if you adopt these words not to use the phrase at any other time, or you may be embarrassed.

Your language list should include the puppy's name, followed by 'come!' Usually, just calling his name will suffice, and you can use hand signals to back up your request. 'No!', said sharply, is a very important word for him to learn – the word that you say when the puppy is about to do, or is actually doing, something that you do not wish him to do.

It is important to make sure that all the members of your family use the same words for the same actions, at least for a year or two. When the dog is an adult and familiar with what he may or may not do, it is possible to vary the commands. However, while he is young he should learn to associate a specific word with the desired action.

Your dog or puppy will enjoy training sessions if you make them fun and keep them short. He will always be ready for walking on the lead!

Reward-based training

Your puppy will soon learn that some things he does will please you and will be rewarded, and this will make him want to repeat them. You must use hand signals and body language as well as words to train him to perform the required actions.

must know

Reward titbits
Dogs respond well to food rewards and it's a good idea when you are training them to keep some small treats in a pocket or your hand. Use dried food, diced cheese or tiny pieces of cooked, roasted liver.

Early days

Training begins at home and from the moment the puppy arrives in your house, he will be learning to interact with you and other members of the family. The message he will receive is that little food rewards and lots of praise come from these people as do mutual play experiences. Life is good with these people and they can be trusted not to hurt or tease him, and to create a secure environment as a foundation for his further socialization experiences.

Rewards

You must always be in control of training sessions. Be patient with your puppy if he does not grasp what you want immediately. He will learn with repetition, so be prepared for gradual progress. It is essential that you reward good behaviour and the correct response with lavish praise and treats. Reward-based training has been shown to be the most effective way of teaching a dog. Smacking a dog or shouting at him when he does not perform the desired action will only make him nervous, confused or aggressive and create behaviour problems in later life. Instead, encourage good behaviour by rewarding it when it occurs. Use specially formulated dried food treats and dog biscuits, or tiny pieces of cheese or liver.

Training guidelines

- Keep the training sessions short. About 10 minutes two or three times a day, preferably just before meals, is enough formal training while your puppy is young, but if you are teaching 'come', every time you need or want to call the puppy is an opportunity for training him.
- Never chase a puppy as a game or because he is annoying you by not coming to your call. The odds will be in his favour as he is likely to be much faster and more agile at dodging your attempts to catch him. The best thing to do in these circumstances is walk away; this takes the advantage away from the puppy, who will find it more rewarding to follow you in the end.
- The same tactics may be applied when an older dog will not return on an off-lead walk. If your dog has this tendency to test your patience, practise calling him and putting him on the lead long before it is time to go home. Praise him, give him a titbit and then let him off after a short time. Repeat this process frequently so that he does not associate the fastening of the lead with the end of pleasure.
- Never use force at any time when you are teaching your puppy the basic commands; it is unnecessary and unproductive.
- Never give your puppy a reward until he has assumed the position or performed the behaviour that you want him to adopt.
- As he learns to comply with your command, do not always give the reward but continue to praise him and show that you are delighted with his behaviour.
- Use the command words you are teaching him often so that the puppy realizes what he has to do to get the reward. Then it's 'good dog', a stroke and a titbit.
- Do remember that in all your training sessions, you must be in control of the situation. Don't allow your puppy to hijack these lessons and turn them into a game. Training must be fun for the puppy to learn, but it has serious goals and it is important that he learns what is expected of him.

'Sit'

It's a good idea to teach this command while your puppy is still young and eager to respond. However, it is never too late to learn and older puppies and adult dogs can still be taught to respond to commands. Teaching your dog to sit will be extremely useful. It will stop him jumping up at people, bothering you when you are busy or eating, and generally make living together easier and more pleasurable.

Your puppy knows the attitude of 'sit'; he has been doing 'sits' spontaneously since he was four weeks old, but what you have to teach him is the word you use when you want him to go into this position. Use rewards to get his attention initially – dog treats are ideal. With practice and patient repetition he will soon learn to associate the word with the required action. The 'sit' is a position that dogs assume readily of their own accord. The head is held high, the front legs are straight, and the hind legs are folded beneath them in a jack-knife position.

When crossing the road with your dog, it is a good idea to teach him to sit on the edge of the pavement and wait for cars to go by before crossing over. This may prevent him getting run over if he ever escapes from your home.

Teaching 'sit'

1 Call your dog by name and attract his attention with a titbit so that he comes to you. You can get down on his level, if wished.

2 Move slowly away, with your hand raised. Keep your dog looking up at your hand. Move a titbit up and back, just above his nose.

3 The dog should go into the 'sit' position naturally because he cannot look up without losing his balance. As his head goes up, his bottom should go down and touch the ground.

4 When his bottom is firmly on the ground and he is in the 'sit' position, praise the dog enthusiastically and reward him with the titbit. Don't offer it unless he is sitting correctly.

Training tips
Never forget that the well-meant use of 'stay' may put your dog in danger if it is misused. Don't leave him in the 'stay' position for long periods; he may bolt into a dangerous situation, be attacked by another dog, or even be 'rescued' by a well-meaning stranger. 'Stay', even when perfected, has limited use for a dog outside the home, but it is a useful ploy to keep him in a static position while you open the front door or move around the kitchen with a hot pan.

'Stay'

When your dog will go into the 'sit' position on your command, you can progress to teaching him to 'stay'. This may be a difficult task as his natural instinct is to be with you, his owner, and you are going to ask him to remain at a distance from you, perhaps in distracting circumstances. If wished, you can put a collar and extending lead on your dog when teaching 'stay', so that you have some control over him. After some patient practice sessions, you will be able to move a metre or so away, or even further, and the dog will be comfortable that he still has the security of your presence even though you are standing a short distance from him.

Useful guidelines

Don't just leave your dog sitting in the 'stay'. You must give the command 'come' to break the 'stay', or the dog may wander off. If he 'breaks' before you have released him from 'stay', then take him back to the position he was in originally and start the exercise again. You may wish to enhance the reward by offering more praise or a better titbit when your dog remains correctly in the 'stay' position, so that he realizes that complying with your wishes is worthwhile. Formally break the control by using some release words of your choice – 'come' or 'OK' will do. Later on, you may want to introduce a distraction, such as another person or dog coming on to the scene, to test your dog's obedience.

If you intend to train your dog up to competitive obedience level, he must learn to 'stay' in one position for 15–20 minutes, probably along with other dogs but with their owners out of sight.

Teaching 'stay'

1 Begin with the dog in the 'sit' position beside you. Hold your hand up, with the flat of your hand towards him, and give the command 'stay', controlling the dog if needs be by use of a collar and lead every time he attempts to move, although this is not essential if your dog responds well. Praise him if he stays in the position and reward him with a titbit. If he attempts to get up or to move, put him back in the 'sit' and tell him firmly to 'stay'.

2 When your dog gets used to remaining in the 'stay' position on command and will stay like this for a few minutes without moving, you can move just one pace or two away from him and continue giving the 'stay' signal. Keep eye contact with him all the time and praise and reward him with a titbit when he complies. As he becomes more obedient and proficient, you can gradually increase the distance between you until you are out of sight. To break the 'stay', call him to you and reward him.

Training tips
If your dog is really
naughty about coming
when he is called, try
putting a collar on him
and attaching a long line
or a piece of rope to it.
When he takes no notice
of your call, gently haul
him in towards you by
means of the line. Praise
him and give him a titbit
within seconds of his
arrival. He must learn
that coming to you
when you call him will
lead to good things.

'Come'

Coming when called is probably the most important
command for your dog to learn. Success always pays,
and if your dog comes straight to you when you call
him, welcome him enthusiastically with cries of
pleasure. Stroke him but without raising your hand
above his head – a young puppy may perceive this
as a frightening gesture. Quickly reward his good
behaviour with a tiny food treat – keep titbits hidden
and out of his way in your pocket or a bum bag.

If your dog does not come to you when you call
him, say nothing but walk away to another place and
call him again from there. Remember that you are
more clever than him, so never let him think that
he can defy you or evade you. Nor should you ever
get cross, shout or punish a dog, no matter what he
has done. Your job is to make training both fun and
rewarding and to persuade him that it is worth his
while to get the task right. Dogs learn by finding out
what behaviour pays best for them.

Timing is essential

Remember that rewards work only if they are given
within seconds of the dog doing what you have
asked him to do. Five minutes later is too late, as
the dog will not then connect what he did with the
gaining of a reward, and you may end up rewarding
behaviour that you did not wish him to do. For the
same reasons, you should never scold your dog after
the event. If you come home and discover a pool of
urine on the kitchen floor, it is useless to shout at the
dog – he will not understand and may think that you
are displeased to see him. Unless you catch him in
the act, scolding him later will only be confusing.

Teaching 'come'

1 Ask a friend to hold your dog for you. Tell him to 'sit' and let him sniff your hand within which you have hidden a tasty treat.

2 Move slowly away, with your hand raised. Keep your dog's attention meanwhile – he should be looking at your hand.

3 Call your dog to you by saying his name or the command 'come' at the same time as you crouch down on the ground at his level, which is similar to an invitation to play.

4 Your friend can now release your dog who should run towards you. Praise him when he reaches you to hold his attention and give him the titbit as a reward for good behaviour.

must know

Training tips
When you have taught your dog the 'down', 'sit', 'stay' and 'come' commands, he will have mastered the basics of training, and you can then elaborate on them as you wish. Remember that you and your dog will learn together, so congratulate each other when you get it right. Even when you get to this stage you cannot stop – training continues throughout your dog's life and he will continue learning into old age.

'Down'

This is the next command to be taught. To achieve this position, the puppy is required to fold his back legs in the 'sit' position and then extend his front legs until they are parallel with the ground. His neck is extended and his head held high. This is another 'resting' pose which the dog does not mind taking up when he understands what you want him to do.

It is important to limit the words that you use and always to employ the same ones to avoid any confusion. They must also be used in the correct context; take care not to say 'down' when you mean to reprimand a dog that is jumping up to greet you. Your dog must get accustomed to a precise word of command for each action he performs.

Like the 'sit', this command needs to be repeated many times and in different situations before it is engraved on your dog's mind and the required action becomes second nature to him. However, the 'down' is easy to practise, wherever you may be.

Body language
Remember the importance of body language in training your dog and raise your hand, palm towards him, to reinforce the fact that he must stay in the 'down' position until you give your command to release him. He will then receive a reward. Try varying the rewards you give to keep your puppy interested.

Puppies learn body movements and hand signals more rapidly than spoken words. To make it easier for your dog to learn the required words, it is beneficial to combine them with a hand signal, at least initially. As he becomes more familiar with the command, you can stop using the hand signal altogether.

Teaching 'down'

1 Start off by asking the dog to adopt the 'sit' position, holding a titbit just above his head. Let him sniff the hand that is holding the treat to keep him interested.

2 Gradually lower and draw back the hand holding the reward, bringing it slowly down between his legs. Keep the reward within your dog's field of vision throughout.

3 As you lower your hand, say 'down' firmly. The dog should move his front legs forwards until his elbows touch the ground in the correct position. Praise him and give him the reward.

4 Teach your dog to stay in the 'down' position until you are ready to release him. Tell him to 'stay' and use your hand with the palm facing downwards to reinforce this.

Walking on a lead

A well-behaved dog should walk quietly by your side on a lead, without pulling too far forwards or deviating backwards or from side to side. No responsible owner should allow their dog to walk without any lead control on any type of road, even on quiet country lanes. It is essential that you train your dog from the earliest possible age to walk happily on a lead at your side. If your dog is a pleasure to walk, you will both enjoy going out together and you will receive mutual benefit from getting more exercise.

Make your dog a pleasure to walk

Get your puppy accustomed to wearing a collar – it can be leather or nylon. Never use any form of chain collar as jerking on a check or choke chain can do serious damage to a dog's throat and larynx. For a few days, just attach a lead to your puppy's collar and let it trail loosely behind him while he is walking round the garden with you. Try to make the lead seem pleasant and fun, not something that your puppy feels obliged to fight. Start more formal lead training either inside the house or outside in the garden before venturing out in public together.

It is essential that you are always in control of these sessions. Never allow your dog to drag you in the direction he wants to go – use your weight to stop this happening. If your dog is to walk correctly on the lead at your side without pulling, the lead must never be tight. If it is taut he will lean into his collar and drag you along behind. If you feel the lead growing tight, stop immediately. Your dog will halt, too. Ask him to 'sit' at your side, and when you are ready to move on, start walking again.

must know

Training tips
When you have taught your dog to focus on walking by your side, introduce a command to remind him – use the word 'heel' or 'here'. He will learn to associate the action with the command. When he is walking steadily, use the 'sit' command when you meet someone coming in the opposite direction or a loose dog rushes up to you. Keep your dog in the 'sit' position and reassure him until the other dog is reclaimed by his owner.

Teaching lead walking

1 Start off by holding the lead in your right hand, with your dog on your left side. Lure him into position with a titbit.

2 Encourage him to move forwards at a normal pace, and praise him enthusiastically when he starts trotting along beside you.

3 Keep checking the lead. If it goes tight or the dog stops, pulls backwards or forwards or veers off in another direction, stop walking and ask him to 'sit' at your side.

4 Praise him when he is in position, give him a titbit to reward him and then start walking again. Offer him titbits regularly as you go along to reward his good behaviour.

'Fetch'

This action comes naturally to many dogs; you can start your puppy playing retrieving games as early as eight weeks old. Mastering this command brings many benefits: retrieving games are fun and good exercise for an energetic dog; the dog will bring back toys to you and relinquish them; and it enables you to build a good relationship with your dog – with you in control of the games being played.

As always, keep the sessions short and be patient with your dog. Retrieving a toy is a complicated process for him with many different elements, and it may take time for him to master it. He needs to know that if he brings it back to you correctly, he will be rewarded with a game and possibly a titbit, too.

Keep it fun

Dogs learn faster and more easily when the training sessions are fun. Playing 'fetch' is an exciting game and they enjoy playing it. Praise and encourage your dog when he brings back the toy and say 'drop' in a light, happy voice so that he knows that this is play.

If he is reluctant to come back to you and runs off with the toy, use a long cord attached to his collar and gently pull him in. Alternatively, to lure him to you, try crouching down at his level, offering a small edible reward in your hand and then praising him effusively when he gives you the toy. However, most dogs are eager to come to the person who has taken over as their foster-mother or pack leader.

When the playtime is over, put away the toy in a safe place, such as a drawer or cupboard, out of the dog's sight; this will make him more interested and keen next time you play a retrieving game.

Training tips
You can develop the retrieve indoors further by throwing the toy into a 'difficult' position – under a cupboard or on to a low table. Your dog must find the toy by scent. Don't forget to use a happy voice and happy face to greet him. Even if he has not carried out a command as well as you would wish, never get angry or lose your temper. Training a dog is a lesson in owner control, too!

Teaching 'fetch'

1 Show the dog an interesting, lightweight soft toy which he can pick up and carry easily. Make sure he gets the scent of the toy.

2 Now throw the toy a short distance across the ground and give the command 'fetch'. Encourage the dog to chase it and pick it up.

3 When the dog picks up the toy, praise him and encourage him to bring it back to you. You can run backwards to tempt him to follow you and say 'come'.

4 When he brings the toy back to you, don't grab it out of his mouth. Praise and stroke him and ask him to 'drop' it before taking it gently from him. Reward him, if wished, with a titbit.

'Drop'

Whenever your dog succeeds in bringing a thrown or requested object back to you at your command, never go into 'tug of war' mode. It may be a precious object that you want back in one piece! Instead, praise him enthusiastically for coming back to you and encourage him to give it to you without having to fight him for it. If wished, you can reward him with a favourite titbit when he complies.

1 When your dog brings an object or toy back to you at your command, don't try to take it from him or pull it out of his mouth. Instead, praise him lavishly for his obedience and then tell him firmly to 'sit'.

2 When he is sitting, put your hand on the object and say 'drop'. As soon as he gives it to you, praise him and reward him with a titbit. If it is a toy and you're playing a game, reassure him that it is safe for him to give it to you.

'Bed'

Sending a dog to his bed should never be used as a punishment. Dogs love their beds and should regard them as a safe place where they can lie and sleep undisturbed, or sit and watch in safety. If you want him out of the way, say 'bed' firmly to your dog, but always use a happy voice and give him a titbit or a favourite toy and praise him when he has settled. Make the bed comfortable with a rug, 'vetbed' or a fleecey blanket, and position it in a draught-free place which is out of direct sunlight.

'Hi five'

Offering a paw is a very endearing action and your visitors will dote on a dog who gives them a paw in a handshake gesture. You can teach your dog this trick and he will enjoy performing it. Ask him to 'sit' in front of you and gently stroke the hairs at the back of one of his front paws until he lifts the foot. Say 'give a paw' and then reward him lavishly with praise and a titbit when he offers it to you. Always practise this command from the 'sit' position. As he gets more proficient and does it naturally when asked, you can raise your hand higher so that he has to stretch his paw up to give you a 'hi five' as you lower your hand.

'Find'

Your dog will enjoy games of hide-and-seek in the house or garden. Show him his favourite toy and throw it out of sight, holding on to his collar. Let go and tell him to 'find' the toy. Reward him when he brings it back to you. As he becomes more proficient, progress to hiding the toy in advance and asking him to 'find' it. He will enjoy looking for it.

want to know more?

• To find out more about training a dog, read Gwen Bailey's *Good Dog Behaviour*, which is published by Collins: www.collins.co.uk
• Read *Collins need to know? Dog Training* for advice on how to make your dog an obedient and happy companion.

weblinks

• To find details of dog trainers and training classes that use positive training methods, log on to the Association of Pet Dog Trainers website at www.apdt.co.uk
• For information on training a puppy and problems you may encounter, log on to www.puppyschool.co.uk

5 Good dog behaviour

When a dog becomes a member of your family, you want him to be acceptable to everyone who visits your home, and well behaved wherever he may be – travelling in the car, walking on the street or running in the park. He has to learn good manners, and you must instil these in him – by obedience training and patient repetition, watchfulness for instinctive behaviour which has to be controlled, and by teaching him to trust you. To be successful, you need to understand your dog's senses and body language, and how to recognize problem behaviour and treat it.

Communicating with your dog

The dog is probably the best communicator in the animal world; perhaps this is why, for thousands of years, dogs have been the favoured companions and workmates of the human race.

Early dogs

From the very earliest days of the canine/human relationship, dogs were not only used to help people with hunting, guarding and herding but were also regarded with great affection. This relationship is validated by a skeleton, which was dug up, of an elderly human, clasping the skeleton of a puppy of about five months. These remains were discovered at a burial site in Israel where the grave was dated as 12,000 years old. It may be that the puppy was actually a tamed wolf. However, it has now been established by scientists that all modern dogs are descended from wolves which indirectly offered themselves to our ancient ancestors as suitable candidates for domestication by becoming part of a human community.

The man/dog relationship

Professor James Serpell wrote in his book *The Domestic Dog* that all the archaeological evidence indicates that the dog was the first species to be domesticated. There were mutual advantages for both dogs and humans – the wolf that came in from the cold instinctively helped man in hunting, pulling down quarry and tracking wounded animals. In return, gradually relinquishing its wild state, the wolf gained the benefit of shelter and food and, eventually, shared company and a tolerable pack

Dogs are faithful companions for children as well as adults. Owning a dog teaches them how to be caring and responsible people.

leader. However, it is unlikely that many wolves were domesticated in this way. Those wolves that did form a relationship with primitive tribes would have mated with other like-minded wolves.

Many generations of mating within this small gene pool would have gradually produced an animal that bore little resemblance physically or temperamentally to the wild wolf; the dog was emerging as a separate and individual animal. And the dog has never left man's side, at least in the Western world. Where there is a break in the dog-man relationship now it is brought about by man's intransigence, never by the dog choosing to be wild again.

Although some dogs may, on impulse, run away from their homes, whether they are compelled by an over-riding desire to seek

We have taken over the role of pack leader and in return for shelter and food, dogs give us their loyalty and affection.

must know

Pack leader
Your dog will become a
member of your human
family pack. Dogs like
to live in a hierarchical
structure and to know
their place within it, like
the members of a wolf
pack in the wild. It is
very important for your
relationship that you
establish yourself as the
pack leader. Your dog
will respect you and feel
secure, knowing that
you are taking care of
his needs and ensuring
that he is comfortable
and happy in the pack.

a willing mate, or to revel in chasing some quarry,
these dogs will invariably return home, provided they
have not been injured in a road traffic accident. A dog
who has temporarily lost touch with his owner through
yielding to the temptation to chase some prey will
usually return to the place where they were last
together, or to the car park where the walk started.
Few dogs want to be on the run permanently, even
when they come from cruel and neglectful homes.

In Britain and across most of Europe, there are no
wild dogs or feral dogs – dogs that have deliberately
chosen to live and breed far away from the homes
that once sheltered them, as feral cats choose to do.
Dogs rarely change homes voluntarily, by leaving one
and applying at another for food and shelter, as some
cats do. So can this special relationship and devotion,
as strong as ever today, be reinforced by the ease
with which man and dog communicate and the
pleasure that both species take in their exchanges?

A unique friendship
The reason why many families have pets is because
the dog can become the confidant of the whole
family. Children can gain a tremendous amount
of comfort and stability from having a canine best
friend who shares their disappointments, troubles
and misunderstandings yet never blames them,
reveals their secrets or transfers his allegiance to
any other person. This unique friendship is especially
valuable in the modern world where many traditional
human relationships are no longer permanent. The
high level of mutual communication that we have
with our dogs is the basis of real friendship on a
special level between dogs and their owners.

**Opposite: The relationship you
have with your dog is unique and
can be a rewarding experience
for both of you.**

Vocal communication

Dogs have an extraordinary vocal repertoire and can talk to us in many ways. Some breeds are more vocal than others, especially Terriers, smaller breeds and German Shepherd Dogs.

must know

Talking to your dog
The way in which you say things to your dog is often more important than what you say. Dogs can interpret your mood from your tone of voice, so you should alter the tone to communicate praise, pleasure, anger or urgency. Your dog will become adept at judging your mood and what you are trying to convey to him in words. Your tone of voice will help you to speak his language and will also help him to understand yours.

Canine sounds

A dog's vocalizations range from a murmur, usually directed straight to the human ear, through to a whine, a pleading bark, a warning bark or aggressive bark, an attention-seeking bark, a low growl or a very deep intense growl, and also a muted howl ranging in intensity over several notes.

Howling

The classic long howl is usually made from a sitting position with the dog's head and throat thrown back into an almost vertical line so that the voice travels as far as possible. It is thought to be a rallying call to the canine pack, which is triggered by separation problems. Dogs do not howl when they are in pain – a dog suffering physical discomfort from an injury is almost always completely silent.

Murmuring

The murmur, made with mouth closed and straight into the human ear, is a demonstration of greeting and affection. Enjoy this spontaneous expression by your dog; he won't murmur to a stranger or someone he does not trust to handle him gently. Puppies in the nest murmur into the dam's ear, which is usually turned back to allow access; the puppy relaxes the outer flap of its ear, a sign of pleasant submission. All puppies are born without hearing although they can vocalize at birth, using the humming murmur for pleasure and satisfaction, usually while feeding from their dam, and also telling the world when they are unhappy, hungry, cold or ill by using a thin, high-pitched wail. The ear canals do not develop until nearly three weeks after the birth. As soon as the puppies can hear they start to use their voices, ranging through sharp little barks at the arrival of the breeder and food, to growls and mini-roars when playing competitively with their littermates.

Whining

This is used to ask you to fulfil a need or wish, such as opening a door or handing out treats. Enjoy the fact that your dog is communicating with you and you can interpret what he is asking for. You will not want to comply with every wish, but when you do, try to make it a happy time because your dog asked and you understood what he wanted. If the request is obscure, make an effort to find out what he wants. You will get a positive response of tail wagging and dancing on hind legs when you find the key to the pleading whine. Less vocal dogs will stand and stare silently at the object they want made available.

Barking

All dogs bark but when they bark obsessively it can be very annoying and a sign that something is wrong. This problem behaviour is usually linked to fear or nervousness, loneliness or attention seeking when dogs feel that they are being ignored. In the wild, barking is used to warn the pack of any threat and also to deter the predator or threat.

You will come to recognize the sounds your dog makes and learn to understand what he is trying to tell you. His body language will also provide clues.

Hearing

Howling in response to a loud noise or a particular musical sound, such as a strident trumpet or violin, may indicate that the noise is actually painful to a dog's very sensitive hearing.

A dog's hearing is very sensitive, and many breeds will prick up their ears and swivel them round to locate sounds.

Sound sensitivity

Remember that dogs can hear much better than us. Their ears are more acute and more discerning than ours. Sound sensitivity of this degree may often coincide with a fear of fireworks and thunder.

Dogs can hear sounds on a much higher register than we can appreciate – in the ultrasonic range – so very high-pitched sounds can actually inflict pain. Dogs will often show fear and resentment, even anger, at household appliances which make a painful sound for them. Breeds with pricked-up, wide-open ears, such as German Shepherd Dogs, can suffer acutely in homes where the television and music are played at a very high volume. Dogs can hear things long before we humans can, such as their owner's car approaching from some distance away.

Fear of thunder is made more acute if an owner is also nervous of the noise; being brave and not reacting to storms will help your dog. Because his first instinct is to run away from an overpowering sound, you should provide a refuge when you know a storm is on the way or neighbours are going to let off fireworks. A covered crate will insulate the dog from the noise, as will access to a bedroom perhaps where he can dive under the bed. Try not to act with any urgency or fear; always stay calm, and then your dog will imitate your mood.

Deafness

Some puppies are born deaf, either in one or both ears – white-coated dogs are more likely to be affected by this inherited fault, and even partially deaf dogs should not be bred from. Susceptible breeds, including Dalmatians, Border Collies, white Bull Terriers and white Boxers, should be tested as puppies before they are sold at eight weeks old.

The old-fashioned way of testing by dropping a tin dish behind a puppy is too inaccurate to be of any use – the puppy may see the movement or feel the air vibration as the testing object falls. The definitive computerized test, called the Brain-stem Auditory Response Test, is quite painless and can be used on puppies from five weeks of age onwards. Your veterinary surgeon can refer you to a specialist in testing for hearing capacity.

Living with a dog who is deaf

You can communicate with a deaf dog through hand signals and body language. He will soon get used to reading your face and interpreting what you want him to do. Even stone-deaf puppies can be trained, by the patient use of human facial expressions, hand gestures, body language and rewards, to be happy and safe companions.

White dogs, such as this cute Boxer puppy, are susceptible to deafness. If you suspect that a dog is deaf, ask your vet about the hearing tests available.

Elderly dogs

In their old age, dogs may lose some of their hearing capacity just as humans do, or chronic ear disease may have the same effect, but these dogs will usually know everything they need about their owners and their way of life, so partial deafness is not a tragedy for them. You will have to be patient if they take time to respond.

Sight

Dogs who live in a human family keep their eyes on their owner all the time. They cannot see colours and differentiate between them as well as humans, but they have a greater field of vision which enables them to see things to the sides and rear.

A dog's eyes are very expressive and are almost always on you. Respond with a smile and you will see his face soften.

Opposite: Dogs, such as Pugs, with protuberant eyes need to be careful as they become scratched and ulcerated easily.

Visual communication

As an owner, you have made, as your ancestors did long ago, a mutual agreement with your dog to live and work together. Your life has no secrets from him; even a half-asleep dog is well aware of everything you do and is poised to accompany you. Unless a dog has a sight defect, he can usually see better than humans in dim light or darkness. At a distance, dogs see moving objects best, so if you are calling your dog from a long way away, use hand signals.

Can dogs smile?

When you catch your dog's eye, you will notice that his whole face softens: the lips spread instead of being tense, and the ears drop. It does you good to smile back, and even if you are not very happy at the time, the knowledge that your dog has sympathy and comfort to offer you can be helpful and cheering.

Staring at dogs

A long, hard stare right into a dog's eyes is a challenge signal and should be used only when it is obvious that he is about to do something that is normally forbidden. Never 'hard stare' an angry or hostile dog or one who is defending his territory. It is better to watch the dog with an oblique glance while planning your next move.

Scent and smell

Dogs have an incredible sense of smell – about 50 times better than ours. Scenting is very important to a dog's way of life and is his way of gathering information about the world and the people and other dogs he meets. Dogs can detect and identify a variety of different scents at very low concentrations.

Scent marking

Dogs live in a different sensory world from us. Not only do they learn about their environment and the other animals and people who pass through it by savouring the distinctive scents left behind on the ground, but they also habitually do their own scent marking by depositing urine and faeces and leaving traces from the sweat glands on their feet. When another dog inspects such a scenting post, it is like a human being reading the local newspaper; he instantly finds out which animal has been that way, how old he was, what sex, where he was going, for what purpose and whether the passing animal was looking for a mate, for food or a burrow.

By appreciating the importance of scent to your dog, you will understand him better and realize why he sometimes behaves oddly, or so it seems to you. He will always sniff, rather than look at, new people, dogs and things that he encounters.

The scent of you, his owner, and the rest of the household are important to him, and a useful means of recognition of familiar people in different clothes or unusual places. This talent is utilized by search and rescue dogs who are given a scent-clue by sniffing the sweat on a garment worn by the victim.

must know

'Counter-signing'
Where several dogs live together in the same household, the leader of the dog pack will 'counter-sign' urine deposits made by the other dogs, so they all urinate on the same patch. This behaviour is part and parcel of the social hierarchy within the dog pack, as the dog with a perceived higher rank urinates last to imprint his scent over that of the other dogs in the pack. This can be a problem if males live together and mark out their territory, especially within the house.

Human footprints also emit individual smells, and an adult dog can successfully follow a trail on grass up to four hours after it was laid. Many dogs seem to dislike strong perfume, perhaps because it masks the natural scent they need to recognize.

This Parson Jack Russell male has picked up a scent in the grass and is following it, even though it may be several hours old.

Rolling in smelly substances

Some dogs, especially Terriers, seem to enjoy rolling in extremely smelly substances, much to the dismay of their owners. This behaviour may be a form of scent camouflage which dates back to when their hunting ancestors needed to disguise their own scent to hunt their prey more successfully.

Body language

Dogs rely to a great extent on body language to communicate with each other and with us. Whereas we use words to make our intentions and emotions clear, dogs resort to body posture and you can learn a lot about your dog by watching him closely.

This little Terrier is happy, alert and confident as he rises into an erect posture on his hind legs to greet his family and visitors.

Reading the signs

By regular observation of your dog's body language, postures and facial expressions, you will be able to find out more about his behaviour and character and learn to recognize what he is trying to communicate to you. There are some universal postures that most dogs adopt, as outlined below.

Happy posture

A happy dog appears relaxed and calm and wags his tail, and sometimes his rear end, too, in greeting when he sees you. He may even press back his ears and pull back the corners of his mouth in a smile.

Fearful posture

A fearful dog will look defensive with his head high, ears drawn back and his tail down. He may pant or yawn excessively and show the whites of his eyes. The pupils may be wide open with a reddish tinge. In some dogs, the hackles along the spine are raised.

Confident posture

A confident dog has an erect posture, holding his head and tail high. He will be friendly, self-assured and popular with other dogs and people. He does not need to use aggression to get what he wants.

Submissive posture

A submissive dog will often curl up small or roll over on to his back in the presence of a dog or person whom he perceives as superior within the pack.

Aggressive posture

An aggressive dog often adopts a still, rigid posture before he attacks. He may stare hard at the object of his anger, his pupils may dilate and his hackles rise.

This King Charles Spaniel is adopting an aggressive posture and is defending his food bowl.

Playful posture

A playful dog will often drop down into a 'playbow' with his front legs flat on the floor and his rear end raised and tail wagging frantically.

Dogs need tails

It has been customary for some dogs to have their tails docked as puppies, either for reasons of fashion and appearance or because they are working breeds whose tails may get damaged. However, thankfully, this practice is now being outlawed and fewer dogs are having their tails docked. A dog with a full tail, as nature intended, possesses a very valuable means of communicating with humans as well as other dogs.

Tail positions

A tail can be wagged in pleasure, particularly when greeting someone, but if it is held out stiffly behind a dog it usually denotes an aggressive posture. When a dog with a tail that is normally 'teapot handle style' is truly and happily relaxed, the tail will straighten out, all except for the last tiny curl.

must know

Warning signs
Tail wagging is not always a sign of friendliness and may indicate that the dog is excited. Indeed, before some dogs bite, they may wag their tail stiffly aloft. A tail that is carried low usually denotes unhappiness or anxiety.

Curing problem behaviour

As dog owners, we have the capacity to create some behaviour problems in our pets. We ask so much of them as companions and want them to share our lives and our homes, but we also expect these pack-orientated animals to be content to be alone when we do not want their company. This causes problems.

Doing what comes naturally

Many aspects of dog behaviour which we perceive as problems are totally natural for dogs and we need to understand why they behave in specific ways if we are to live together in harmony. For instance, we may wish a dog to warn us of intruders but we don't want him to create any unnecessary noise. When he fails to live up to the canine image we have created, we say he has a behaviour problem, meaning that he does not always behave in the way we expect.

A new industry of animal behaviourists has arisen around the need to stop dogs doing what comes naturally to them – chewing, gnawing, barking and urine marking on the dwarf conifers. It is possible to modify some of a dog's more annoying behaviour traits if we try to analyse what is causing the behaviour and why the dog finds it necessary to do it. Whatever the problem is, it's not done to annoy us.

Being a good owner

A good owner will take the initiative to establish a good relationship with their dog and promote and reward desirable behaviour from an early age. Mutual trust and respect are essential elements in a successful human/canine relationship. If your dog wants to please you, it is easy to promote and reward his good behaviour. By being aware of the warning signs of unwanted behaviour and taking action to manage them, you are less likely to encounter problems later on. If you stop bad habits forming when your puppy is still young, you can encourage good behaviour and reward him when he gets it right.

Shouting is counter-productive

If your dog behaves badly, shouting at him is nearly always ineffective and will only make him anxious or even frightened of you. This is especially true if he is unsure of the reasons why you are displeased with him and you are punishing him some time after the event that provoked your displeasure. Owners who are in control and effective pack leaders do not need to shout at their dogs; they know how to earn their respect and get their compliance. By rewarding good behaviour when it occurs and training their dogs to respond to the basic commands, they can not only have the joy of owning a well-behaved dog but can also build a relationship which is based on friendship and will last a lifetime. Dogs soon learn that behaviour that is rewarded is worth repeating.

Boredom or lack of mental simulation, especially in active breed types like the Boxer, can lead to destructive behaviour.

Old age

As a responsible owner, you should take account of the disabilities of old age – elderly dogs tend to drink more water and consequently they need to urinate more often and in bigger quantities. If they also suffer from arthritis, they may find it difficult to get up from their beds to go outside, or they may not get to the door in time. Try to be understanding and not to grumble or scold them. Instead, devise a plan to make their life easier for them.

House soiling

If you house-train your puppy effectively at an early age, you should not experience any problems later on. However, you may inherit or adopt a rescue dog who is not house-trained or soils your home due to anxiety and nervousness. Sometimes a dog, who may have been perfectly house-trained for a long time, will suddenly start to urinate or worse in the house, either during the night or when you are out. In order to treat this problem successfully, you need to discover the reasons for the dog's behaviour.

Examine the possibilities

First of all, think illness. Are there any indications that the dog is not well: is he drinking more; does he have diarrhoea; is it inevitable that he cannot wait as long as you expect him to? Can you make it easier for him to get outside when he needs to go? Have you made any changes to his diet? Could the formula of the food you give him have been altered?

Then think disturbance. Have there been visitors or workmen in the house, or another pet introduced? Are there any new noises from your neighbours? Many dogs are creatures of routine and they can be disturbed by domestic changes. Tummy problems may be their way of expressing their anxiety, so watch carefully for a few days and then, if there is no improvement, consult your veterinary surgeon.

Build an outside run

It is a good idea, if possible, to create the means whereby your dog can exit the house into the garden when necessary. You could build a small well-fenced concrete run to which he has access through a dog door. He will soon learn how to use it, and he will have an alternative environment when you are out which is preferable to being shut inside the house.

Take your dog outside regularly

Dogs who are house-trained will want to go to the toilet outside instinctively and will be clean in the house. However, they cannot last for hours on end, and you must let them out first thing in the morning, at regular intervals during the day, after meals and last thing at night before you go to bed. Otherwise, you must be prepared for the inevitable accident. In warm weather, you can leave the doors open to your garden if it is fenced securely and allow your dog to come and go as he pleases.

Male dogs

Some male dogs may perform urine marking indoors if they feel that some provocation warrants it. Scent marking can be triggered by many things: a bitch in season in the house or next door; rivalry or a new member in the family dog pack hierarchy; or even a new baby in the home. In fact, any creature with a completely different smell may trigger off the dog's need to mark the premises as his own.

If it becomes excessive and you think that male hormones may be to blame, neutering may be the answer – your vet can advise you on this. However, if you think the cause is fear or insecurity, you need to identify why your dog is feeling like this and work out what you can do to change the situation. Getting angry with the dog and punishing him will not help. He will not learn from this and it is only likely to make the situation worse.

must know

Cleaning up
You must always clean up all indoor mistakes thoroughly, but do not use an ammonia-based product as this will compound the smell of urine. Supermarkets now sell a range of floor, upholstery and carpet cleaners which are specially formulated for cleaning up our pets' mistakes and they do work very effectively.

Play biting

Many people are disappointed when they want to cuddle and make a fuss of their new puppy but he seems intent on biting them. Although his tiny sharp teeth can inflict quite painful bites, this is normal behaviour and not the portent of an aggressive dog. When you get your puppy at around eight weeks, he should have his first set of baby teeth, but the second – permanent – teeth will be coming through until he is about four months old. Teething pain causes the puppy to need to gnaw, unfortunately often at your furniture or even your hands or ankles. To make teething less painful, offer your puppy some hard nylon bones or edible chews to gnaw on.

Preventing play biting

Puppies can play quite roughly with their littermates but they do need to learn not to treat their human playmates in the same way, however exciting it may seem. Some play bite more than others, especially Terriers and bull breeds, and you must not indulge in rough and tumble games or allow them to bite you or hang onto your clothes. Don't let your children play chase and grab games with the puppy.

Always express your displeasure at hand biting with a sharp 'ouch!', over-exaggerating the pain felt. Giving the puppy something more suitable to bite, such as a tasty chew or a toy, is the best deterrent. When playing with him, hold a toy and keep your hand moving but out of reach of his teeth. Praise him when he is gentle. If he bites your hand, stop the game immediately and put the toy away in a safe place. He must learn that play biting is not beneficial, and playing with a toy is more rewarding.

Edible chews

Treated real bone is ideal for strong, boisterous dogs and keeps them occupied for a long time.

Real hide strips have a strong taste to tempt most dogs but can become smelly over time.

Rawhide strips, bones and toys are ideal, and good for teething as they will not damage a puppy's mouth or teeth and soften easily.

Limit compressed chews and bones as they can upset a pup's tummy and crumble quickly.

Opposite: All puppies go through a spell of play-biting, especially when they are teething. When your puppy bites you, cry out in pain so that he realizes he is hurting you.

Separation anxiety

Some dogs suffer from separation problems and hate being left alone at home. This may be because they are pack animals and isolation is not a natural state for them. When they are left alone they may whine or bark excessively, scratch and chew doors in an attempt to get out and seek their owner, or urinate and defecate in their distress. If your dog suffers from separation anxiety, you need to find an effective way of treating the problem and teach him to get used to being left alone without getting upset.

Training starts in puppyhood

Being alone in a room for a short time is one of the lessons that a puppy should learn in his first weeks in your home. Puppies need periods of quiet and rest, but make sure that the 'time out' is quite short and peaceful and not a punishment for bad behaviour. Tidy up the room before leaving the puppy as he may well chew any object you have recently handled and which smells of you. Alternatively, you can place his

If you leave your dog alone in the house, he may find it comforting to have access to a window where he can watch the world go by and look out for your return.

bed and toys in a playpen. Make his bed comfortable, and leave a soft toy and a nylon chewing bone where they can be found, together with a small untippable bowl of water. Perhaps leave the radio on, tuned to a talk station so that the puppy hears a human voice. Put him in the room, give him a treat and praise him, then quietly shut the door and walk away. Gradually increase these periods of isolation, starting with a short length of time – maybe just a few minutes – and repeating the sessions several times a day.

Your puppy will eventually grow to accept your absences if you keep repeating them and extend the time gradually. If the puppy cries initially when you shut the door, harden your heart and walk away. When he has been quiet for, say, five minutes, open the door and let him out. Your behaviour at this stage is critical, so do not make a great fuss of him. Just treat it as an ordinary day-to-day experience. It is also probably a good idea to follow the 'time out' by going into the room used with the puppy and finding something to do there, so that you and the puppy can be companionable together in a quiet situation and he does not link the room with being left alone.

Make your exit low-key

As the puppy grows, you may need to be away for longer periods. It is important to make your exit and return very low-key and not to say effusive farewells nor greet the dog too enthusiastically on your return. These will only make the dog feel that your absence is a big event. Before you go out, it may be a good idea if you take him out for a walk to exercise him or have a little play session together, but do nothing that will heighten his excitement.

must know

Don't blame the dog
It is never fair to blame your dog for what he has done in your absence, and when you return home it is certainly too late to punish him for something that he may have done an hour ago. So say nothing, but take note and plan what you can do to prevent more damage occurring again in the same place.

Boredom and destructive behaviour

If you leave an active dog alone for long periods, he
will soon become bored and this can trigger various
forms of problem behaviour, including noisy barking
and chewing furniture and other forbidden items.
Terriers and the working breeds may be particularly
affected and are more likely to engage in destructive
behaviour than to lie down quietly and go to sleep.
To prevent this happening, you need to leave your
dog something to do to keep him busy while you are
away. You can then be confident of returning to an
undamaged house and a happy dog.

Solving the problem

Before you leave home for any length of time, make
sure you exercise your dog physically and mentally.
Take him out for a long walk or a run. Play some
games with him or even engage in a training session
together. If he is pleasantly tired after spending some
enjoyable time with you, he is more likely to settle
down happily and will have a sleep or some quiet
time on his own after you go out.

Make sure you leave him some toys or chews and
bones to amuse and keep him occupied during your
absence. Try to provide a new smelly one which will
grab his interest, but remove it later when you come
home. Leaving different chews will not only give him
something to do but it will also make it less likely
that he will chew rugs and furniture if he is bored.

If you are planning to be out for long periods, say,
most of the day, you should arrange for a friend or
neighbour whom your dog knows and trusts to come
in and play with him and also take him out for a walk
and to go to the toilet to prevent mess in the house.

**Opposite: If you go out, don't
leave shoes and other things you
don't want chewed lying around.**

Escaping and roaming

Some dogs, no matter how happy they are at home with their owners, are accomplished escapologists and will take advantage of any opportunity to slip out. This problem is usually sex-related and starts in puberty. Male dogs sometimes escape to get to a neighbouring bitch in season – they can smell one within a three-mile radius. Bitches who come into season may also try to leave home to find a mate. However, some dogs run away because they are anxious or frightened at home, or because life outside appears to be more exciting to them.

must know

Mating partners
Bitches and dogs will both try to escape to look for mating partners. At the end of their season, bitches may roam to find a mate, whereas males can smell a bitch on heat from up to three miles away and may well cover a wide area.

Dealing with the problem

How you treat this problem will depend, of course, on the cause of your dog's behaviour. You need to confirm the reason by finding out where your dog goes and what he does when he is away from home. If your dog escapes in search of a mate, neutering may be the answer, and you should talk to your vet about this course of action.

If he heads for the park or local woods and fields in search of canine or human company, he may be bored at home and seeking excitement elsewhere. If you think that this is the case, make an effort to put aside some time every day to play with your dog. Make these sessions enjoyable for both of you – your dog should be mentally and physically stimulated. Do remember to praise and reward him when he behaves in an appropriate way. You could also try teaching him some simple tricks to exercise his mind or, if you are both very energetic, go along to flyball or agility classes. These are the fastest growing canine sports and exciting for the dog and his owner.

Opposite: Many dogs run away from their owners and refuse to return to them when they are called. To prevent this, take a ball or Frisbee to the park with you.

Jumping up and excitable behaviour

Excitement seems to project a dog into jumping up
towards our faces, just as very young puppies will jump
up to the mouth of their mother to get her to disgorge
food. It is embarrassing and annoying when your dog
insists on jumping up to greet a visitor.

Dealing with the problem

One way to stop your dog jumping up to greet you is
to crouch down to make a fuss of him. Alternatively,
you can take hold of his collar and tell him firmly to 'sit'
before getting down on his level and rewarding him.
If he behaves well with you, he is more likely to be well-
mannered with visitors to your home.

When someone visits your home, you can adopt the
same routine of holding his collar and giving him the
'sit' command to calm him down. However, if he is
really boisterous and excited when newcomers arrive,
you may have to accustom him to being shut in the
kitchen or some other room before letting people in.
Say 'this way' and the dog will troop in, knowing that
he must not be at the front door when it is opened.
It is a good idea to let the visitors enter the house and
sit down, preferably at a table so that they have some
protection when the dog comes in. Ask them not to
interact nor make any eye contact with the dog until
all the excitement has died down. They should not
touch him, speak to him or reward him in any way.

It may be possible that your dog gets over-excited
and hyperactive when people are present because he
is bored and under-exercised. Look at his lifestyle and
exercise regime. Do you spend enough time with him,
playing games and taking him out for walks? Does he
have sufficient toys and chews to keep him occupied?

Jumping up is an annoying habit –
and potentially dangerous if you
happen to own a large, boisterous
dog. Discourage your dog from
jumping up at you, even in play.

Stimulating your dog

Playing games

Your dog is more agile and more clever than you may realize and he will enjoy learning training exercises and playing games. Playing with dogs is fun for us, too; we get so little opportunity for carefree play.

Hide and seek

Dogs enjoy hide and seek, hunt the slipper and other games that stretch their mental powers. Their ability to find hidden objects is well demonstrated by sniffer dogs who can find drugs or guns. Your dog, especially if he is a scenting breed, can specialize in finding objects.

Puzzle solving

Dogs enjoy solving puzzles. As an exercise, block the way through a door with some boxes and then see how your dog works out his own solution to creating an exit for himself. You could set up a mini agility course in your garden, with a flexible tunnel that the dog has to crawl through, a ladder to climb and a suspended tyre to jump through.

Rough and tumble

Wrestling with big dogs seems an irresistible game for the young and fit, but remember that a large dog will always win. It is better not to play rough games or to indulge in tug-of-war contests with dogs with dominant tendencies.

Ending a game

Never end a game in such a way that your dog thinks he has won. Always end when you are ready, saying calmly 'that's enough' or 'finish'. Reward and praise the dog when he stops playing on your command. Never put yourself in competition with the dog when he has all the attributes to win.

Play together every day

Mental stimulation will help to prevent boredom and can stop unwanted behaviour problems developing, many of which may be caused by having nothing to do. Try to make time to play with your dog every day. It will strengthen the bond between you.

Predatory sequence

Sight hounds were bred to look for prey and chase it, while herding dogs were bred to chase and round up livestock in a controlled manner. Both have an enhanced enjoyment of chasing and are attracted to fast-moving objects. The predatory sequence for them is: track; watch; stalk; chase; bite; kill; dissect; and, finally, eat.

Chasing

While it is perfectly acceptable for your dog to enjoy chasing a ball, this is not the case if he likes to chase cyclists, joggers and cats. Herding breeds and sight hounds may often be afflicted with this problem as they are genetically programmed to chase. If your dog enjoys chasing people, other animals or even cars, you must channel his instincts into a more suitable outlet and teach him to chase toys instead.

Cat chasing

Many dogs chase cats because they regard them as legitimate prey. Others just enjoy the thrill of the chase or perceive them as intruders on their territory and want to remove them from their homes and gardens. If your dog has these tendencies, try to prevent neighbouring cats visiting your garden and keep him on a lead when cats are around, praising and rewarding him if he is calm and ignores the cat.

You can channel a dog's chasing instincts into more appropriate behaviour by playing together and throwing a ball for him to chase and bring back to you.

Preventing the behaviour

If your dog likes chasing inappropriate things, you must control him in situations where there may be objects to chase and encourage him to play chasing games with you instead. Throwing a favourite toy or ball for him to chase puts you firmly in control of the situation and provides an acceptable outlet for his behaviour. If he is a hound, he may not wish to participate in these games as he is programmed to chase real moving animals and to kill them when he catches them. This behaviour may be natural to him but you cannot tolerate it and you will have to exercise him in a safe area. You may even need to consider him wearing an open-box style of muzzle.

Some large dogs like to chase smaller dogs and this can lead to fights and injuries. If your dog has these tendencies, encourage him to chase toys and do not allow him to run freely in public places where there may be other dogs.

Effective socialization starts while your dog is still a puppy.

Aggression to other dogs

This is a very common problem for which there are many possible causes. Bad experiences and poor socialization in puppyhood, limited opportunities to interact with other dogs, and a desire to defend owners and territory can all play their part in making dogs behave aggressively towards each other.

Preventing the problem

Effective socialization starts while your dog is still a puppy and you should take him to training classes to mix with a wide range of other dogs. He must have pleasurable experiences with them and enjoy playing together without any bullying or aggression. If your dog is fearful of strange dogs and barks, lunges or growls at them, you should not let him run freely in public places. Exercise him on an extending lead and try to focus his attention on you. Encourage him to enjoy playing with you instead of wanting to approach other dogs, and reward his good behaviour with motivational tasty treats and lots of praise.

Some dogs, especially the guarding breeds, are territorial and aggressive towards dogs who cross the boundaries of their territory. German Shepherd Dogs are particularly prone to this type of aggression. The desire to guard their home is paramount and these dogs react aggressively to visitors and tradesmen as well as other dogs. Socialization is the answer and if the dog is introduced to others on neutral territory to play together, he may be more friendly towards them on his own territory, especially if you praise and reward good behaviour. Most aggression is caused by fear and insecurity; if you can nurture a confident, friendly dog, you won't have these problems.

must know

Bullying
In a multi-dog house, one dog may be weaker and less confident than the other(s) and this can lead to bullying if he behaves submissively. You must keep an eye on the dogs and teach the aggressive dog to play enjoyable, gentle games with you away from the weaker dog. In extreme cases, consult a pet behaviourist or vet.

Aggression to people

If your dog behaves aggressively towards strangers and visitors or even towards you and your family in specific situations, you must take steps to discover what is causing this behaviour and to solve the problem. Dogs act aggressively when they feel that they are threatened. Often they have had traumatic experiences as puppies and were under-socialized. They only feel safe with people they trust and may growl or lunge at strangers.

Resolving the problem

If the dog is still young, it is not too late to conquer his fears and provide lots of enjoyable experiences with a wide range of different people in various situations to make him react in a more confident, friendly way. You can help him by being kind but firm, encouraging and rewarding friendliness and earning his respect. Create a safe environment for him. Body language is important, too – don't tower over him or raise your hand. Get down to his level and approach him from the side, avoiding direct eye contact. By adopting a non-threatening posture, you can encourage him to lose his anxiety and approach you in a more friendly fashion.

Dogs will often become quite boisterous when they play together and may even growl in warning when they are good friends. Often one will roll over in submission.

must know

Guarding food
Some dogs will react aggressively to anyone who comes near them while they are eating. They may growl or even try to bite your hands. You can prevent this in puppies by feeding them separately to avoid food competition and by teaching them that human hands are good news, not bad, and bring treats. For older dogs, you may need to consult a professional.

Car travel problems

It is essential that your dog gets used to travelling by car or on public transport. Whereas some puppies will embrace car travel enthusiastically and want to accompany their owner everywhere, others are fearful and are terrified by the whole experience.

Making the experience fun

If you introduce your puppy to car travel at an early age and make the experience enjoyable, he will be a good traveller. When you bring him home from the breeder, arrange for a family member or friend to cradle him safely in their arms.

A relaxing place

In the first few days, get the puppy accustomed to going in the car – do this gradually. Park the vehicle in the shade and let him explore the car, then sit on the back seat with him. Let him relax or fall asleep. The car must be perceived as a restful place, so keep him calm, as some dogs tend to get over-excited in cars and subsequently behave badly. Take him out as often as you can for short journeys to enjoyable places, so he associates car travel with fun.

Restraining the dog

Decide where the dog will travel when he is older. For large breeds, buy a suitably sized dog crate, which is designed to fit into the luggage area. Your dog will have plenty of room, and the wire construction will protect him in the event of an accident. A smaller dog can ride in a small crate placed on the back seat. Alternatively, consider using a safety harness.

A special car safety harness will restrain your dog comfortably and safely while you are driving.

Curing excitable behaviour

Some dogs get very excited when they travel in cars, jumping around and barking excessively, especially if they spot a passing dog or know that they are going for a run in the park. Wear your dog out with a game in the garden before you leave home. Take him on car journeys that do not always end in a treat. When you reach the park, do some obedience drills to calm him down or sit quietly until he behaves normally.

Car sickness and fearfulness

Dogs who drool or suffer from car sickness are best taken in a car on an empty stomach. When the ride is over they can be fed as a 'reward'. If your dog gets distressed and is sick in the car, do not sympathise or make a fuss. Just clean him up and drive on. In time he should get over these reactions, just like children.

want to know more?

• For a hands-on rescue package for dog owners, read *It's Me or the Dog* by Victoria Stilwell. See www.collins.co.uk

weblinks

• For Gwen Bailey's advice on dealing with dog behaviour problems: www.dogbehaviour.com
• Help on curing a range of behaviour problems can be found at www.dogstrust.org.uk
• To find a pet behaviour counsellor or to attend a seminar or workshop run by the Association of Pet Behaviour Counsellors, log on to www.apbc.org.uk

6 The healthy dog

As a good owner, it is your responsibility to keep your dog fit and healthy. If you follow the basic guidelines in this book and socialize him, feed him a nutritious diet, exercise him adequately, groom him and play with him, you can prevent many health problems. However, it is important that you learn to recognize the warning signs of common problems and diseases so that you can treat them yourself or seek professional help from your veterinary surgeon before they get worse. Prevention is always preferable to cure, and a healthy, contented dog will be your trusted companion for many years to come.

Signs of good health

Examine your dog regularly and check for any warning signs of potential health problems. If you know what to look for, you can prevent ill health or identify tell-tale symptoms early enough to treat them effectively before they become more serious.

Appearance and behaviour

Check your dog over once a week – when you are grooming him is usually a good time to do this. If you handle him in this way from an early age, he won't mind you opening his mouth and peering into his ears and eyes when he grows older and bigger. Look for the following signs:

• A healthy dog should always look healthy and bright-eyed.

• He should be full of energy, always ready for a walk or a game.

• He should not be too fat nor too thin.

• He should have a healthy appetite.

Any changes in his normal appearance, temperament and behaviour should be analysed carefully as they may be clues to present or future health problems. Watch out especially for any persistent scratching and licking, which may be caused by parasites, allergies, injuries or skin inflammation.

Coat
The coat should be in good condition and should smell pleasantly 'doggy'. It should be glossy and pleasant to touch. When you part the hairs, there should be no signs of fleas' droppings, sore or bare patches.

Anal region
This should be clean without any faeces clinging to the fur. The dog should not lick this area excessively or drag his rear along the ground.

Eyes

The eyes should be bright, alert and with no signs of discharge, swelling or tear stains. A tiny amount of 'sleep' in the inner corners is quite normal.

Nose

The nose of a healthy dog should be cold and damp without any discharge. Occasionally there may be a little clear fluid.

Ears

They should be responsive to any sound. The insides should be pale pink with no visible wax or unpleasant smell. Your dog should not shake his head or scratch his ears too often.

Teeth

Healthy teeth are white and smooth, not yellow, which is a sign of plaque and tartar formation. The breath should not smell unpleasant and there should be no loose or missing teeth or inflamed or bleeding gums.

Body

The dog's body should be firm and well-muscled. He should not carry excess weight nor be so thin that his ribs stick out.

Claws

The claws should end level with the pad and not be too long. Look out for broken claws, damage to dew claws (if they have not been removed) and hay seeds embedded in the pads.

Checking for problems

If your dog is feeling unwell or off colour, you will quickly realize that something is wrong. Check him over and if you cannot identify a simple problem you can treat yourself, ring your vet.

When to seek help

The health problems that can afflict dogs are being intensively researched, and we now know much more about how similar and how different dogs are compared to other animals or humans when they are unwell. An intricate machine needs a skilled mechanic, so do not be tempted to tinker with your dog's health. It is both useful and beneficial if you learn to recognize certain symptoms and what you can do about them. You should also be capable of performing simple first aid – with an emphasis on the 'first' – in emergencies. However, it is very important that you seek veterinary help for all but the mildest and briefest conditions.

Self-help

On a practical basis, there is a lot you can do to keep your dog healthy and prevent too many expensive visits to the vet. Vaccinating your dog and treating him for fleas and worms on a regular basis will help as will keeping his ears clean and coat groomed. In all his ailments, whether mild or serious, you may have to be prepared to do something, usually acting as a nurse, and there are some techniques to be learned which are explained later in this chapter, so that you are armed with the knowledge and basic skills to look after a sick dog with loving care.

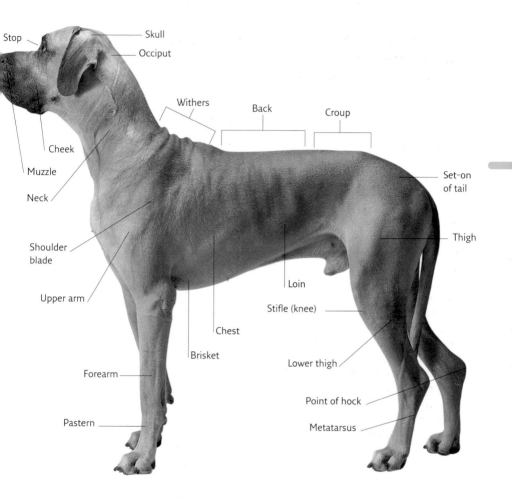

Stop

Skull

Occiput

Withers

Back

Croup

Cheek

Muzzle

Set-on
of tail

Neck

Thigh

Shoulder
blade

Upper arm

Loin

Stifle (knee)

Chest

Brisket

Lower thigh

Forearm

Point of hock

Pastern

Metatarsus

The dog's anatomy

When you read the breed standards compiled by the
Kennel Club or veterinary textbooks, you may come
across some unfamiliar terminology relating to the
dog's anatomy. The main points are annotated on
the image of the Great Dane illustrated above.

**The specialist terminology for
the dog's anatomy.**

Hereditary diseases

As in humans, dogs can inherit a wide range of diseases, and these may occur in pedigree and cross-bred animals. They are caused by genetic faults or aberrations in the breeding line.

Genetic faults

The genetic background to many hereditary ailments can be extremely complicated and is of concern to all professional breeders, veterinarians and geneticists. Screening tests are available for tendencies to some hereditary diseases, and potential owners of dogs, particularly pedigrees, should consult their vet about possible inherited health problems within the breed and ask the breeder about the lineage and history of the dams and sires before purchasing a puppy. Although some hereditary diseases are treatable, the underlying genetic faults cannot be eliminated. Overleaf is some information about some of the best known hereditary diseases with the breeds most commonly affected (see pages 146–147).

Hip dysplasia

This is one of the most common inherited diseases and affects many breeds. In a normal, healthy dog the hip is a 'ball and socket' joint, allowing a wide range of movement. The rounded end at the top of the femur fits tightly into the cup-shaped socket in the pelvis. In hip dysplasia, a shallow socket develops with a distorted femur head and slack joint ligaments. There can be excessive movement between the femur and pelvis, leading to a malfunctioning joint which will gradually become arthritic.

must know

Affected breeds
Hip dysplasia affects some dog breeds more than others, especially German Shepherd Dogs, Labradors, Retrievers and Rottweilers. It is also becoming more common in smaller breeds but does not affect mongrels.

Early symptoms

If a puppy develops severe hip dysplasia he may have difficulty walking. Getting up from a sitting position may be painful and he will cry out. When he runs, he may use both hind legs together in a 'bunny hop' or look as though he's swaying. These symptoms may be identifiable from five months onwards. Mildly affected puppies may show no signs at all of hip dysplasia at this age, but they will begin to develop arthritis at about eight years of age.

Hip dysplasia scheme

The British Veterinary Association and the Kennel Club run a joint scheme (the BVA/KC hip dysplasia scheme) based on hip scoring. The vet submits the X-ray, bearing the KC registration number of the dog, to the scheme. Each hip is then scored from 0 to 54, making a total of 108 maximum between the two hips. The lower the score the better, and 0:0 is the best score possible.

You should not breed from a dog or bitch with a higher hip score than the average for the breed or hip dysplasia will never be reduced or eliminated from that breed. When buying a puppy, check that both parents have been X-rayed, scored, and achieved a low score. This does not guarantee the puppy won't develop hip dysplasia but it does reduce the chances.

Treatment

If mild hip dysplasia is treated in a growing puppy with anabolic steroids, limited exercise and diet, he will often grow into a healthy adult dog. However, you may have to restrict his exercise later on, too. In severe cases, surgery is available.

German Shepherd Dogs are one of the breeds that are susceptible to hip dysplasia. When you buy a puppy, check the score for both hips.

Common hereditary diseases

Disease name	Nature of disease	Breeds most commonly affected
Bone/skeletal diseases		
Hip dysplasia	Deformation of hip joint	Labrador, other Retrievers, German Shepherd
Elbow dysplasia	Deformation of elbow joint	German Shepherd, Afghan Hound
Osteochondrosis dessicans	Disease of joint surfaces, particularly shoulder	Larger breeds, including Border Collie, Golden Retriever, Great Dane, Labrador Retriever
Wobbler syndrome	Malformation of neck bones	Great Dane, Dobermann
Eye diseases		
Entropion	Inturned eyelids	Many breeds but particularly Shar Pei
Ectropion	Out-turned eyelids	Clumber Spaniel, St Bernard
Cherry eye	Enlargement of gland in third eyelid	American Cocker Spaniel
Progressive retinal atrophy (PRA)	Degeneration of retina with progressive loss of sight	Irish Setter, Springer Spaniel
Collie eye	Another degeneration of the retina	Collie, Shetland Sheepdog
Glaucoma	Increased pressure within the eye	American Cocker Spaniel, Poodle
Cataract	Cloudiness of lens in the eye	Poodle, Labrador Retriever, Golden Retriever, American Cocker Spaniel, Beagle
Cardiovascular diseases		
Subaortic stenosis	Narrowing of the aorta with effects on heart	Boxer, German Shepherd, German Short-haired Pointer, Newfoundland
Pulmonic stenosis	Narrowing of pulmonary artery with effects on heart	Beagle
Ventricular septal 'hole in the heart' defect	Heart defect	Bulldog
Patent ductus arteriosus	Heart defect	Poodle, German Shepherd, Collie, Shetland Sheepdog, Pomeranian
Bleeding disorders		
Haemophilia	Clotting defects	Many breeds
Von Willebrand's disease	A special form of haemophilia	Golden Retriever, German Shepherd, Dobermann and Scottie

Disease name	Nature of disease	Breeds most commonly affected
Neurological diseases		
Cerebellar atrophy	Degeneration of the cerebellum in brain	Many breeds, including Rough Collie, Kerry Blue, Gordon Setter
Deafness		Border Collie, Boston Terrier, Bull Terrier, Collie, Dalmatian, English Setter, Old English Sheepdog
Hydrocephalus ('water on the brain') and epilepsy		Both can occur in many breeds and they are suspected of having a genetic cause
Hormonal diseases		
Hypothyroidism	Underactive thyroid gland	Beagle, Dobermann, Golden Retriever
Cushing's Disease	Overactive adrenal glands	Poodle

Preventing disease

Prevention is always better than cure and there is a lot you can do to prevent diseases and health problems developing by keeping your dog in first-class condition. Get into the habit of inspecting and looking after his ears, eyes, teeth, coat, paws and rear end.

must know

Stimulate your dog
Playing games with your dog and teaching him tricks will provide both mental and physical stimulation. Lively dogs need to be busy and active, or they soon become bored and this can lead to behaviour problems as well as to poor health.

Check your dog

On a regular basis - a grooming session is a good opportunity - examine your dog. Look inside his mouth, checking that his teeth are clean and white and his breath does not smell unpleasant. Clean the teeth with special toothpaste at least once a week.

Next check his eyes, nose and ears for signs of any discharge, odour or inflammation. Keep them clean by wiping gently with some damp cotton wool.

Examine the dog's coat, looking for bald patches, excessive hair loss, tell-tale signs of fleas (black sooty specks in the fur) and soiling around the anus and rear end. The coat should look healthy and glossy, and the dog should not scratch excessively.

Pick up each of his paws and check the pads and claws, which should not be broken nor too long. If your dog appears to be limping, look for cuts or any swellings on the pads. Some dog breeds, especially Spaniels, are susceptible to grass and hay seeds becoming embedded in their pads.

If you find anything unusual or suspect there may be a health problem, then make an appointment to take your dog to the vet. Even if it is only a minor worry, this will set your mind at rest. You can treat the problem before it gets more serious and learn how to prevent it recurring in the future.

Diet is important

Feeding a balanced, nutritious diet will help to keep your dog healthy. It is important not to over-feed him or he may gain too much weight and this can lead to many health problems that are associated with obesity as well as a reduced life expectancy. If you are unsure as to which foods, how much and how often to feed your dog, ask your vet. Similarly, if your dog loses his appetite or sheds weight suddenly, ask your vet's advice – the dog may well need worming (see page 152) or the symptoms may be a sign of a more serious problem.

Keep your dog fit and active

All dogs need regular exercise every day to keep fit and stay in optimum health. The amount and type will vary according to the breed. Thus an active working breed, such as a Collie or Springer Spaniel, should walk and run many miles a day, whereas a toy breed, like a Pug, may be happy with a stroll round the garden and a walk round the block.

All dogs love to run freely off the lead. Give your dog as many opportunities for exercise as possible, depending on the breed. He will be healthier and happier if he stays fit and active.

Parasites

Dogs can play host to two sorts of unwelcome parasite: external and internal ones. By worming your dog regularly and treating him with flea treatments, especially in the spring and summer, you can prevent infestations occurring and keep him healthy.

External parasites
(Not to scale)

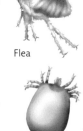

Louse   Flea

Sarcoptic   Tick
mange mite

External parasites

These parasites live on the surface of the dog's body, and include lice, fleas, ticks, mites and ringworm (see page 172). Keep a look out for them and treat an infected dog as quickly as possible.

Fleas

Dogs are usually infested by their own, and the cat's, species of flea but sometimes they can carry rabbit, human or hedgehog fleas. The infestations are more likely to be worse in warm weather in the summer, but fleas thrive all the year round, particularly if your home has central heating. Sometimes it is extremely difficult to find any fleas on a dog, but just a single flea can cause an allergic reaction when piercing a dog's skin and injecting its saliva. Such a reaction can result in widespread irritation, skin sores and rashes. Flea eggs do not stick to the dog's hair like those of lice (see opposite), but, being dry, they drop off onto carpets and furniture.

Common symptoms
- An affected dog will keep scratching.
- Tiny reddish scabs or papules appear on the skin, particularly on the dog's back.
- Flea droppings look like coal dust in the coat.

What you can do

Use insecticidal sprays, shampoos or powders, which are obtainable from the vet, chemist or a pet shop, at regular intervals throughout the summer. Treat the floors, furniture and your pet's favourite sleeping places, basket and bedding with a specially formulated aerosol product every seven months. This procedure effectively stops the re-infestation of dogs by larvae emerging from eggs in the environment.

Lice

There are two kinds: biting lice which feed on skin scales; and sucking lice which draw tissue fluids from the skin. The latter cause more irritation to the dog than the former. Lice are greyish-white and about 2mm (^{1}/8in) in length. Their eggs (nits) are white and cemented to the dog's hairs. The dog louse does not fancy humans or cats and will not infest them.

Common symptoms

- The dog will scratch himself.
- Lice and nits will be visible to the naked eye when the dog's coat is carefully searched.

What you can do

Sprays, powders or baths are available from the vet or pet shop. Apply on at least three occasions at five- to seven-day intervals to kill adults and the larvae that hatch from the nits.

Ticks

More often seen on country dogs than town dogs, ticks suck blood, their abdomen swelling up as they do so. The commonest tick of dogs is the

When using flea spray, remove and spray the dog's collar, and then spray the dog, making sure you protect his eyes and mouth as you do so.

Specialist tick tweezers are useful for removing these little beasts. Avoid squashing the tick and releasing its fluids or leaving any part of the head in the skin as both may cause infection. Afterwards use some disinfectant on the affected area.

sheep tick. It clings to the dog's hair, generally on the legs, head or under-belly, and pierces the skin with its mouth parts. In doing so it can transmit an organism called *Borrelia*, a cause of Lyme Disease. Characterized by lameness and heart disease, it requires veterinary diagnosis by means of blood tests, and then treatment using specific antibiotics and anti-inflammatory drugs.

What you can do

Remove a tick by dabbing it with some alcohol, such as gin or methylated spirits, waiting a few minutes for its head to relax, and then grasping it near to the mouthparts with fine tweezers – you can buy special ones (see left). Dislodge the tick with a little jerk. Do not ever pull it off without applying the alcohol first as the mouthparts left in the skin may cause an abscess to form.

An alternative method is to spray the tick with some flea spray and then to remove it the following day. The regular application of a flea spray or fitting your dog with an insecticidal collar during the summer months is highly recommended in order to control tick infestation.

Internal parasites

These parasites live inside the dog's body. Several kinds of worm can infest dogs and, in very rare cases, these parasites can spread to human beings.

Roundworms

These live, when adult, in the dog's intestines but their immature forms migrate through their host's body, damaging such organs as the liver and lungs, particularly those of puppies.

Hookworms and whipworms

These blood-sucking parasites can cause severe anaemia. Your veterinary surgeon will be able to confirm if your dog is affected.

Tapeworms and roundworms

The commonest dog tapeworm, *Dipylidium*, is spread by fleas, in which its larvae develop. You can see the segments of this tapeworm looking like wriggling white grains of rice in droppings or stuck to the hair around the dog's bottom. Roundworms cause the most trouble for dogs, particularly puppies.

Common symptoms

• Symptoms of roundworms include bowel upsets, emaciation, fits, chest and liver malfunction.
• Tapeworms may cause dogs to drag their rear ends ('scoot') along the floor.

What you can do

To treat roundworms you should give your dog a 'worming' medication which will be available from your vet. Puppies usually should receive their first dose at three weeks of age. Repeat the worming every three weeks until they are 16 weeks old, repeating at six months and twice a year thereafter.

Give your dog anti-tapeworm medication once a year or when any worm segments are seen in his droppings or on the hair near and around the anus. Regular flea control will also help you to combat tapeworms. Some worm treatments are effective against all types of internal parasites, and you should consult your veterinary surgeon about which products are suitable and the correct dosage.

Internal parasites
(Not to scale)

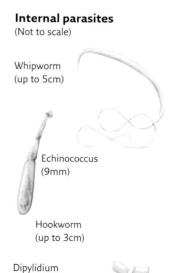

Whipworm
(up to 5cm)

Echinococcus
(9mm)

Hookworm
(up to 3cm)

Dipylidium
(30–40cm)
Usually single sections are seen stuck around the dog's bottom

Dental care

Check your dog's teeth regularly and brush them once or twice a week to prevent any tartar building up. Gnawing on a variety of bones and chews will help keep his teeth clean and healthy.

At the vet's

Canine dentistry is easily tackled by your vet. Using tranquillizers or short-acting general anaesthetics, tartar can be removed from a dog's teeth with scrapers or an ultra-sonic scaling machine. Antibacterial drugs may be prescribed if encroaching tartar has caused secondary gum infection. Bad teeth must be taken out to prevent root abscesses and socket infection from causing problems, such as septicaemia, sinusitis or even kidney disease, elsewhere in the dog's body.

Tooth disease

It is relatively easy to spot the common symptoms of tooth disease and dental decay.

Common symptoms

- Your dog may salivate (slavering) at the mouth.
- He may paw at his mouth.
- His chewing motions may be exaggerated.
- He may chew tentatively as if he is dealing with a hot potato.
- His breath may smell unpleasant.

What you can do

Cleaning the teeth once or twice weekly with cotton wool or a soft toothbrush dipped in salt water (or specially formulated dog toothpaste) will stop tartar formation. 'Bones' and 'chews' made of processed hide (available from pet shops) and the occasional meal of coarse-cut, raw butcher's meat also helps.

Tartar

When tartar, a yellow-brown, cement-like substance, accumulates, it does not produce holes in the teeth that need filling. Instead it damages the gum edge, lets in bacteria to infect the tooth sockets and thus loosens the teeth. Tartar always causes some gum inflammation (gingivitis) and frequently bad breath.

If your pet displays the symptoms described, open his mouth and look for a foreign body stuck between his teeth. This may be a sliver of wood or bone stuck between two adjacent molars at the back of the mouth or a bigger object jammed across the upper teeth against the hard palate. You can usually flick out foreign bodies with a teaspoon handle.

Periodically check the lip pouch on soft-mouthed dogs, such as Cocker Spaniels, as they may contain leftover food which can cause bad breath and infection.

Gingivitis

Bright red edging to the gums where they meet the teeth, together with ready bleeding on even gentle pressure, are the principal signs of gingivitis (gum disease). Tap each tooth with your finger or a pencil. If there are any signs of looseness or tenderness, wash the dog's mouth with some warm water and salt, and give him an aspirin tablet – there is little else you can do without seeking professional help. Take the dog to the vet and ask his advice.

Broken teeth

Sometimes a dog will break a tooth, perhaps by fighting or chewing stones (a bad habit that some dogs get into). The large 'fang' teeth (canines) are most often the ones damaged. These injuries do not usually produce any signs of toothache, root infection or death of the tooth. Treatments used in human dentistry, such as fillings, root treatments or crowning, may be necessary and are all possible.

Ulcers and tumours

Mouth ulcers, tumours (juvenile warts are common in young dogs) and tonsillitis will all need veterinary diagnosis and treatment where they are the cause of some of the symptoms mentioned above.

Eye problems

Your dog's eyes are precious and you must check regularly that they are normal and healthy. Breeds with protuberant eyes, such as Pugs, can be especially prone to eye injuries and ulcers.

Watering and discharge

If just one of the dog's eyes is involved and the only symptom is watering or a sticky discharge without any marked irritation, you can try washing the eye gently with boracic acid powder in warm water once every few hours, followed by the introduction of a little Golden Eye ointment (which is obtainable from the chemist) onto the affected eyeball.

If any symptoms in or around the eyes last for more than a day, you must take the patient to the veterinary clinic and get professional treatment. Particularly in young dogs, two mattery eyes may indicate distemper (see page 162).

Eye conditions

Persistent watering of one or both eyes can be due to a very slight infolding of the eyelid (see opposite), or to blocked tear ducts. A blue or white film over one or both eyes is normally a sign of keratitis, which is an inflammation of the cornea. This is not a cataract but it does require immediate veterinary attention. Opacity of the lens (cataract) can be seen as a blue or white 'film' much deeper in the eye. The pupil looks greyish in colour instead of the usual black. This usually occurs in elderly dogs but it may be seen sometimes in young puppies (congenital cataract) and also at other ages (diabetic cataract).

Inflammations of the eye

These can be treated by the veterinarian in a variety of ways. Antibiotic injections, drops and ointments are available, plus various other drugs to reduce inflammation, as are surgical methods of tackling ulcerated eyes under local anaesthesia. Problems due to deformed eyelids, foreign bodies embedded in the eyeball and even some cataracts can all be treated surgically nowadays.

Entropion

In this inherited disease, which affects several breeds of dog, including Labradors and German Shepherd Dogs, the edge of the eyelid folds inwards so the lashes rub against the eyeball itself. The eye becomes sore and weeps and may be kept closed. The condition can be corrected with surgery.

1 To apply eye ointment, hold the tube parallel to the eyeball and pull the lower eyelid down slightly. Let 1cm (½in) of the ointment fall onto the eyeball or inside the lower lid.

2 Now hold both the dog's eyelids closed for five seconds to allow the ointment to melt and begin dispersing. It is important to master this technique to apply ointments effectively.

Ear problems

A healthy dog's ears should be alert and responsive to sounds. The ear flaps of most breeds are usually pale pink and silky inside, and there should be no wax or nasty odour. A dog who keeps scratching his ears and shaking his head may have an ear infection.

Preventing problems

Clean your dog's ears once a week. For breeds with hair growing in the ear canal (e.g. Poodles or Kerry Blues), pluck out the hair between finger and thumb. Don't cut it. Using 'baby buds' or twists of cotton wool moistened in warm olive oil, clean the ear with a twisting action to remove excess brown ear wax. See the vet early with any ear trouble. Chronic ear complaints can be very difficult to eradicate.

Treating minor problems

If symptoms suddenly appear and the dog is in distress, an effective emergency treatment is to pour a little warmed (not hot) liquid paraffin carefully into the affected ear. Acute inflammation will be greatly soothed by the oil. Don't stuff proprietary liquids into a dog's ear; you do not know what you may be treating. Most of all, avoid those so-called canker powders as the powder bases of these products can cause additional irritation by forming annoying accumulations that act as foreign bodies.

Ear irritation

This may be due to various things that find their way into the ear canal. Grass awns may need professional removal. Small, barely visible white mange mites that live in dog's ears cause itching, and bacteria can set up secondary infections. Sweaty, dirty conditions, particularly in the badly ventilated ears of breeds like Spaniels, provide an ideal opportunity for germs to multiply. The vet will decide whether mites, bacteria, fungi or other causes are the source of inflammation, and will use antiparasitic, antibiotic or antifungal drugs as drops or injections.

Middle-ear disease

Although tilting of the head may be due simply to severe irritation on one side, it can indicate that the middle ear, the deeper part beyond the eardrum, is involved. Middle-ear disease does not necessarily result from outer-ear infection but may arise from

Check your dog's inner ear flap once a week and carefully pluck out any unwanted hair.

Dogs may get grass seeds lodged in their ears if they walk in long grass. Check the ears afterwards.

To remove any surface wax from a dog's ear, gently use some twisted cotton wool. If the dog is holding his head to one side, you may suspect a foreign body in the ear. If so, seek your vet's help.

trouble in the Eustachian tube which links the middle ear to the throat. This will always require some rigorous veterinary attention with the use of antiflammatory drugs, antibiotics and, more rarely, deep drainage operations.

Ballooning of an ear flap

This may look dramatic and serious but in fact it is a relatively minor problem. It is really a big blood blister, which is caused by the rupture of a blood vessel in the ear flap. It generally follows either some vigorous scratching where ear irritation exists or a bite from another dog. It can be treated surgically by the vet, who may drain it with a syringe or open it and then stitch the ear flap in a special way to prevent any further trouble.

Nose problems

Don't allow your dog's nostrils ever to get caked and clogged up. Bathe them thoroughly with warm water and anoint the nose pad with some soothing cold cream. If there are any 'common cold' symptoms, you must seek veterinary advice immediately.

Sore noses

Old dogs with cracked, dry nose pads need regular attention to keep their nostrils free and to deal with bleeding from the cracks. Bathe the nose frequently, applying cod liver oil ointment twice or three times daily and working it in well. Your vet may prescribe multivitamins or corticosteroid preparations.

Rhinitis and sinusitis

Sneezing, a mattery discharge from the nostrils, head shaking and, perhaps, nose bleed may indicate rhinitis (the inflammation of the nasal passages) or sinusitis (inflammation within one or more of the sinus chambers in the skull). Bacterial, viral or fungal germs, foreign bodies, growths, tooth abscesses or eye disease can be the cause.

Like humans, dogs possess air-filled spaces in the bones of their skulls (sinuses) which can become diseased. Infections or tumours can occur in these cavities. Sometimes an infection can spread into them from a bad tooth root nearby. The signs of sinusitis include sneezing, persistent nasal discharge and head shaking. If you notice these symptoms, take your dog to the vet. The treatment can involve anti-bacterial or anti-fungal drugs, surgical drainage or dental work as appropriate.

must know

Common symptoms
- The dog's nostrils are running and mattery
- The dog appears to have the equivalent of a human common cold
- The nose tip is sore, cracked and dry
- Check the eyes as well as the nose – if they are both mattery, the dog may have distemper

Respiratory problems

Dogs can suffer from bronchitis, pleurisy, pneumonia, heart disease and other chest conditions. Coughing and sneezing, the signs of a 'head cold', possibly together with mattery eyes, diarrhoea and listlessness, may indicate distemper – a serious virus disease.

must know

Common symptoms
- The dog may cough
- There may be some wheezing and sneezing
- The dog's breathing may be laboured

Distemper

Although this is more common in younger animals, it can occur at any age and shows a variety of symptom combinations. Dogs catching distemper can recover although the outlook is serious if there are symptoms such as fits, uncontrollable limb twitching or paralysis, which suggest that the disease has affected the nervous system. These may not appear until many weeks after the virus first invades the body.

What you can do

Your dog should be vaccinated against distemper at the first opportunity – when he is a puppy – and make sure that you keep the annual booster dose going. At the first signs of any generalized illness, perhaps resembling 'flu' or a 'cold', contact the vet. Keep the dog warm, give him plenty of liquids and provide easily digestible nourishing food.

Your vet will be able to confirm whether the dog has distemper. Because it is caused by a virus, the disease is very difficult to treat. Antibiotics and other drugs are used to suppress any dangerous secondary bacterial infections. Vitamin injections will help to strengthen the body's defences. The debilitating effects of coughing, diarrhoea and vomiting are countered by drugs which reduce these symptoms.

Coughs

Where troublesome coughs occur in the older dog, give a half to two codeine tablets three times a day, depending on the animal's size, but see the vet.

Heart disease

This is common in elderly dogs and often responds well to treatment. Under veterinary supervision, drugs can give a new lease of life to dogs with 'dicky' hearts. It is useful in cases of heart trouble and in all older dogs to give vitamin E in the synthetic form (50–200mgm per day depending on thedog's size) or as wheat germ oil capsules (two to six per day).

Bronchitis

Inflammation of the tubes that conduct air through the lungs can be caused by a variety of bacteria and viruses, parasitic lungworms, allergy, inhalation of dust, smoke, foreign bodies or excessive barking. Specific therapy is applied by the vet and sometimes, in the case of foreign bodies, surgery or the use of a fibre-optic bronchoscope is necessary.

Pneumonia

There are many causes of pneumonia in dogs, the commonest being infections by micro-organisms such as viruses or bacteria. Migrating parasitic worm larvae and inhalation of foreign bodies are less frequent. The signs are faster and/or more laboured breathing, a cough, raised temperature and, often, nasal discharge. It can be treated with antibiotics, corticosteroids, 'cough' medicines and medication to relieve symptoms. Pneumonia always demands immediate professional attention.

must know

Kennel cough
This is caused by a bacterium (*Bordetella*) or viruses (Canine parainfluenza virus, Canine herpes virus or Canine adenovirus) or a mixture of these. The signs are a dry cough, often with sneezing, and a moderate eye and nostril discharge. Dogs can be protected by special vaccines administered either by injection or, in some cases, as nasal drops.

Tummy problems

There are numerous causes for tummy troubles in a dog but if you are worried or the symptoms persist for longer than twelve hours, you should consult your veterinary surgeon. If your dog has a minor tummy upset, you could try feeding him some rice or pasta cooked with chicken, or some other bland meal.

must know

Common symptoms
- An affected dog may experience vomiting, diarrhoea, constipation
- There may be blood in the dog's droppings
- The dog may lose his appetite and refuse food
- Flatulence may be present
- The dog may eat or drink more than normal
- He may drink less than he normally does

Vomiting

Vomiting may be simple and transient due to either a mild infection (gastritis) of the stomach or to food poisoning. If severe, persistent or accompanied by other major signs, it can indicate serious conditions, such as distemper, infectious canine hepatitis, an intestinal obstruction, leptospirosis or a heavy worm infestation. In this case, seek veterinary attention urgently. The usual treatment for vomiting is to replace lost liquids (see *diarrhoea* below) and give the dog one to three teaspoons of Milk of Magnesia, depending on his size, once every three hours.

Diarrhoea

This may be nothing more than the result of a surfeit of liver or a mild bowel infection. However, diarrhoea can be more serious and profuse where important bacteria are present, in certain types of poisoning and in some allergies. Again, you should take your dog to the vet as soon as possible.

For mild cases of diarrhoea, cut out solid food, milk and fatty things. Give your dog fluids – best of all are glucose and water or some weak bouillon cube broth – little and often. Ice cubes can also be supplied for licking. Keep the animal warm and indoors.

Constipation

If your dog is constipated and is not passing any stools, it may be due to age, a faulty diet including too much chomped-up bone, or to an obstruction. Don't use castor oil on constipated dogs. Give liquid paraffin (a half to two tablespoons). Where an animal is otherwise well but you know he is bunged up with something like bone which, after being crunched up, will set like cement in the bowels, you could get a suitable enema from the chemist.

All dogs eat grass – it is normal behaviour – but sometimes it may indicate a tummy problem, and the dog is trying to vomit.

Blood in the stools

This condition can arise from a variety of minor and major causes. It may be from nothing more than a splinter of bone scraping the rectal lining, or the cause may be more serious, such as the dangerous leptospiral infection. Your vet will be able to identify the cause and advise on suitable treatment.

Malabsorption

Some dogs with chronic diarrhoea (often rather fatty looking), associated with a strong appetite but loss of weight, are not able to digest or absorb their food normally. The causes include enzyme deficiency (liver or pancreas faults) or disease of the bowel walls.

Giving your dog a healthy, well-balanced diet will help to prevent many common tummy problems.

The vet will employ a variety of tests to establish the cause and prescribe the appropriate therapy. Dogs deficient in pancreatic enzymes can be given pancreatic extract supplements with their food.

Polydipsia and polyphagia

Both of these conditions – polydipsia (drinking more than normal) and polyphagia (eating more than normal) – can be associated with diabetes, disease of the adrenal glands, kidney disease and other conditions. Careful examination of the patient by the vet, together with laboratory tests on blood and/or urine samples, is necessary to pinpoint the cause and thus lead to the correct treatment.

Salmonella infection

Salmonella is a type of bacterium that occurs in a wide variety of strains (serotypes) which may cause disease in, or be carried symptomlessly by, almost any species of animal. Sometimes salmonella can be found in the droppings of apparently normal healthy dogs. Dogs can contract salmonellosis by eating infected food, especially meat and eggs, or by coming into contact with rodents or their droppings, other infected dogs or, more rarely, reptiles or birds. The most common symptoms include diarrhoea (sometimes bloody), vomiting, stomach pain and even collapse, sometimes ending in death.

Diagnosis is confirmed by the vet sending away some samples for bacteriological culture and identification. Treatment is by means of specific antibiotics and fluid replacement. However, it is worth remembering that salmonella infection in animals may be transmissible to humans.

must know

Acute abdomen
The sudden onset of severe pain, vomiting with or without diarrhoea and the collapse of the dog into shock is an emergency that necessitates immediate veterinary attention. The cause may be a powerful, rapidly-developing infection, obstruction of the intestine by a foreign body or a twist of the bowel itself, torsion (twisting) of the stomach, acute kidney, liver or uterine disease or poisoning. Successful treatment depends on quick diagnosis.

Urinary problems

Male dogs will urinate many times a day, in the course of a walk or a run in the garden. Bitches generally urinate less often. The usual signs of urinary disease are increased thirst and urination.

Types of urinary disease

If something is wrong with your dog's waterworks, see the vet. Inflammation of the bladder (cystitis), stones in the bladder and kidney disease are quite common and need immediate professional advice. Whatever you do, don't withhold drinking water.

Leptospirosis

This is the most common disease of a dog's kidneys. Humans can be infected by contact with dogs who suffer from this. Symptoms can be acute with loss of appetite, depression, back pain, vomiting, thirst, foul breath and mouth ulcers, or more chronic with loss of weight and frequent urination. It can be diagnosed by blood and urine tests and treated with antibiotics. Vaccination is also available.

Cystitis

This inflammation of the bladder generally responds well to effective treatment with antibiotics, such as ampicillin, perhaps together with medicines that alter the acidity of the urine and urinary sedatives.

Calculi

A diagnosis of stones (calculi) in the urinary system can be confirmed by your vet. In most cases, they are easily removed surgically under general anaesthetic.

Opposite: Your male dog may urinate frequently during the course of a walk but it is more likely due to territory marking than a urinary problem.

Skeletal problems

The most common skeletal problems in dogs are arthritis and slipped disc. Arthritis is much more common in elderly dogs than in young ones, and it invariably follows hip dysplasia.

Arthritis

This painful condition may arise from the congenital weakness of certain joints, their over-use/excessive wear, injuries, infections and nutritional faults. Treatment is similar to that in humans, and your vet may well prescribe corticosteroids, non-steroidal anti-inflammatory drugs and various analgesics.

Massages, perhaps with anti-inflammatory gels or creams, homoeopathic remedies and acupuncture can also afford relief and improved mobility in some cases. If you are considering trying out alternative medical treatment, consult your vet first.

You should avoid taking your dog out in very cold or wet weather, and buy him a snug coat for outdoor use. Provide daily multivitamins and minerals and give elderly dogs, in particular, one to four capsules or teaspoons (depending on size) of halibut liver oil.

Obesity

Carrying excess weight can put extra strain on a dog's joints. Slim down an overweight dog by modifying his diet (reducing carbohydrates and fats), feeding special canned slimming rations, desisting from giving him sweet titbits, and increasing his exercise gradually. Your vet may run a slimming programme: expert guidance will be provided and your dog's progress will be monitored by regular weighing.

Slipped disc

The dog's adjacent spinal vertebrae are separated by discs shaped rather like draughts pieces, which act as shock absorbers when functioning correctly. With the passing of time, as dogs grow older, the discs lose their elasticity and become more brittle, less compressible and degenerated. Then, a sudden movement or trauma can cause a disc to 'burst' with the discharge of crunchy material that piles up against the spinal cord or a nerve root with the consequent rapid onset of symptoms. The disc itself does not actually 'slip' out of line with the spine. Certain dog breeds, particularly ones with relatively long backs for their size and short legs, such as Dachshunds, Basset Hounds and Pekingeses, are more likely to suffer from disc prolapse.

must know

Painful joints
Arthritis can result in the thickening of the joint capsule, abnormal new bone forming round the joint edges, and wearing of the joint cartilage. The joint is enlarged and painful and its movement is restricted. It tends to affect the shoulders, hips, elbows and stifles.

Symptoms and treatment

The signs of a slipped disc include sudden onset of neck or back pain, paralysis or weakness of the limbs, loss of sensation, limb spasms and loss of control of the bladder. Accurate diagnosis is aided by X-rays. Treatment is by means of medication (analgesics, sedatives, anti-inflammatory drugs and anabolic hormones) and, in some instances, surgery to relieve the pressure on nervous tissues. Good nursing by the owner of the dog under veterinary advice is essential for the animal's recovery.

Slipped disc is more common in the long-backed breeds, such as the Dachshund.

Skin problems

There are many kinds of skin disease that can affect dogs, and their diagnosis needs examination and often sample analysis by the vet. If you suspect skin problems, seek expert advice.

must know

Common symptoms
• Thin or bald patches in the coat
• Scratching; wet, dry or crusty sores

Mange

This can be caused by an invisible mite and can be seen as crusty, hairless sores. Fleas, lice and ticks all cause damage to a dog's coat (see page 150). If you see or suspect the presence of any of these skin parasites, you must obtain a specially formulated antiparasitic product from the pet shop, chemist or your vet and treat your dog immediately.

Powders are of little use against mange, and drugs in bath or aerosol form are more appropriate. Tough, deep forms of mange, such as demodectic mange, may be treated by your veterinary surgeon using a combination of baths and drugs given by mouth.

As there are several different types of mange, you should ask the vet to advise you on the best method of treating your particular case. With all anti-parasite treatment of skin diseases, it is extremely important that you follow the instructions on the label of the preparation being used.

Ringworm

This subtle ailment, may need diagnosis by ultra-violet light examination or fungus culture from a hair specimen. Special drugs, which are given by mouth or applied to the skin, are used for ringworm. Care must be taken to see that human contacts do not pick up the disease from the affected dog.

West Highland White Terriers suffer from their fair share of skin problems. Ask your vet if your dog has any particular problem relating to his breed.

Lumps and bumps

These may be abscesses, cysts or tumours and they may need surgical attention if they persist and grow larger. The earlier a growing lump is attended to, the simpler it is to eradicate, so you must consult your vet by the time it reaches cherry size.

Hot spots

Sudden, sore, wet 'hot spots' that develop in summer or autumn may be caused by an allergy to pollen and other substances. Use scissors to clip the hair over and round the affected area to a level with the skin, and apply liquid paraffin. Consult your vet as the dog may need anti-histamine or corticosteroid creams, injections or tablets. Although they look dramatic, hot spots are quickly settled by treatment.

Nursing a sick dog

In all your dog's ailments, mild or serious, you will normally have to be prepared to do something to look after his welfare, usually acting in the capacity of nurse. This will involve learning some essential nursing techniques, such as how to take the animal's temperature and administer tablets and liquid medicines.

Taking your dog's temperature

You cannot rely on the state of a dog's nose as an effective indicator of his temperature, good health or sickness. As with children, being able to take your pet's temperature with a thermometer can help you to decide whether or not to call the vet and can also assist him in diagnosing and treating what is wrong.

You should use an ordinary glass thermometer, which you can purchase at most pharmacies. For preference, it should have a stubby rather than a slim

Liquid medicine can be poured into the dog's mouth or syringed direct into the lip pouch. This will ensure that all of the medication is administered properly.

bulb, or, better still, you can invest in an unbreakable thermometer, although these are more expensive.

Lubricate the thermometer with a little olive oil or petroleum jelly and insert it about 2.5cm (1in) into the dog's rectum. Once it is in place, you can hold the thermometer with the bulb angled against the rectal wall for good contact. After half a minute, remove and read the thermometer.

A dog's normal temperature will be in the range of 38–38.6°C (101–101.6°F). Taking into account a slight rise for nervousness or excitement in some dogs, you can expect under such conditions to read up to 38.7°C (101.8°F) or even 38.8°C (102°F). Higher than that is abnormal. Shake down the mercury in the thermometer before use, and be sure to clean and disinfect the instrument afterwards.

Administering medicine

Try to avoid putting medicines into your dog's food or drink, as this can be a very imprecise method. However, for dogs that are really averse to pills and capsules, you can conceal them in tasty titbits, but you must check that the dog has swallowed them.

Tablets, pills or capsules

These should always be dropped into the 'V'-shaped groove at the back of the dog's mouth while holding it open as illustrated (right), with one thumb pressed firmly against the hard roof of the dog's mouth.

Liquids

These should be given slowly, a little at a time, by the same method or direct into the lip pouch with the mouth closed. They can be squirted through a syringe.

Giving a tablet

1 To give a tablet, hold the mouth open and then drop it into the 'V'-groove at the back of the mouth.

2 After giving a tablet, whether by hand or applicator, massage the throat to help it on its way. An alternative method of giving pills is using a water-filled pill gun which 'shoots' the pill from a syringe with a dose of water to aid swallowing.

Handling your dog

It is very useful to know how to handle and restrain your dog effectively during visits to the vet, especially if he gets anxious about being examined or may even behave aggressively.

1 Tie a knot in the bandage and wrap it around the dog's muzzle.

2 Cross the ends of the bandage at the bottom under the jaw.

3 Bring the ends round to the back of the dog's head and tie firmly.

Making a makeshift muzzle

A muzzle is essential when a nervous, possessive, aggressive or sensitive dog is in pain and has to be handled or examined. To make one, you can use a length of bandage, string, nylon stocking or even a tie – it will prevent the owner and vet being bitten.

By carefully positioning the muzzle not too far back, you can still administer liquid medicine by pouring it into the gap between the lips behind the encircling band.

At the vet's

It is important to know how to handle your dog when you visit the vet's surgery. Although some dogs trot in happily and do not mind being examined, others can be nervous and may even panic.

Very large dogs are usually looked at on the floor, but the vet will want to examine small to medium-sized dogs on the examination table and you will have to lift your dog up if so.

Lifting your dog

To avoid injury, not only to your dog but also to your back, always bend your knees when picking him up. Support his body properly with one hand on his chest between the front legs and the other below his rear (see opposite).

Lifting your dog

1 If lifting a medium-sized dog, bend your knees and place one hand securely under his rear and the other around his chest.

2 With your hand at the rear, taking most of the dog's weight and holding him securely, rise onto one knee, keeping your back straight.

3 Keep the dog in a secure position, holding him close to your body, then rise to your feet, bringing him up to chest height.

First aid

First aid is the emergency care given to a dog suffering injury or illness of sudden onset. The aims of first aid are to keep the dog alive, avoid unnecessary suffering and prevent further injury.

Accidents and emergencies

Common accidents and emergencies require you to have a basic knowledge of first aid. In emergencies, your priorities are to keep your dog comfortable until he can be examined by a vet. However, in many cases, there is important action you can do immediately to help preserve your dog's health and life.

Burns

These can be caused by very hot liquids or by contact with an electrical current or various types of caustic, acid or irritant liquid. You must act quickly.

Electrical burns

Most electrical burns are the result of a dog chewing a live flex or cable, so wires should always be hidden, particularly from puppies, and electrical devices unplugged after use. Biting live wires can cause burns to the inside of the lips and the gums but may, in the worst cases, result in shock, collapse and death.

Recommended action

First, switch off the electricity before you handle the patient. Examine the insides of the mouth and apply cold water to any burnt areas. If the gums are whiter than normal or blue-tinged, shock may be present. You must seek veterinary advice.

To treat chemical burns, wash the affected area immediately with copious warm soapy water before taking the dog to the vet.

Chemical burns

Burns can be caused by caustic chemicals, and you must seek veterinary attention if this happens.

Recommended action

Wash the affected area of the coat with copious warm soapy water and then seek veterinary advice.

Scalding with a liquid

Hot water or oil spillage commonly occurs in the kitchen. Although the dog's coat affords him some insulating protection, the skin beneath may well be damaged with visible signs only emerging after several hours have passed in many cases.

Recommended action

You must apply plenty of cold water immediately to the affected area and follow this by holding an ice pack on the burn – a bag of frozen peas is ideal. Then gently dry the burnt zone with mineral oil (liquid paraffin) and seek veterinary advice.

To treat burns, you must apply lots of cold water and then follow this by holding an ice pack or frozen peas pack on the spot.

Poisoning

The house, the garden and the world outside contain a multitude of substances, both natural and artificial, that can poison a dog. If you suspect that your dog has been poisoned, you must contact your vet right away. Frequently some symptoms, such as vomiting, blood in the dog's stools or collapse, which owners may imagine to be the result of poisoning, are actually caused by other kinds of illness.

A dog may come into contact with poisonous chemicals through ingestion or by licking his coat when it is contaminated by a noxious substance. Canine inquisitiveness and the tendency to scavenge can lead dogs to eat or drink some strange materials. Sometimes owners will negligently give dangerous substances to their pets. Occasionally, poisonous gases or vapours are inhaled by animals.

Types of poison

All our homes contain highly poisonous compounds, including weedkillers, pesticides (rat, slug and insect killers), fungicides, disinfectants, car antifreeze, lead compounds, caustic cleaning fluids, paint thinners, creosote and excessive amounts of patent medicines, such as paracetamol and aspirin. Poisoning can also be caused by certain plants, insect stings and the venom of snakes and toads.

Poisonous plants

Dangerous plants include the bulbs of many spring flowers, holly and mistletoe berries, the leaves and flowers of rhododendrons and hydrangeas, leaves of yew, box and laurels, sweetpea, wisteria and bluebell seeds, and all parts of the columbine, hemlock, lily of the valley and ivy. Some fungi are as poisonous to dogs as they are to humans, as are the blue-green algae that sometimes bloom on garden ponds in hot weather. Keep your dog away from these plants.

Common symptoms

The symptoms of poisoning vary but they may be evident as digestive upsets (especially vomiting and diarrhoea), difficulty in breathing, convulsions, uncoordinated movements or even coma. If any of these occur in your dog and you suspect poisoning, you must ring the vet immediately.

Flush out the dog's mouth carefully with some warm water. Let him drink water or milk if he will take it.

Recommended action

Determining which poison is involved can be quite difficult if you don't know what the dog has come into contact with. Professional diagnostic methods at the earliest opportunity are vital. Look for any evidence of burning or blistering in the dog's mouth caused by corrosive poisons. Flush out the mouth with warm water and let him drink water or milk.

In the case of corrosive substances, wipe clean the contaminated area with rags or paper tissues and cut off congealed masses of hair with scissors. Cooking oil or petroleum jelly will help soften paint and tar. Wash thoroughly with dog or baby shampoo and rinse well. Don't use paint thinners, concentrated washing detergents, solvents or turpentine.

If the poison has been swallowed recently (within one hour) then try to make the dog vomit by giving him either a hazelnut-sized chunk of washing soda (sodium carbonate) or some English mustard powder (a level teaspoon in half a cup of water for a medium-sized dog, and pro rata).

must know

Snake bites
Britain's only venomous snake, the common adder, may sometimes bite a dog who disturbs it. The bite produces two tiny slit-like punctures in the skin which rapidly become surrounded by a zone of swollen reaction. An affected dog may tremble, salivate, vomit and stagger, and then go into shock and collapse or even die. You must take him straight to the vet for treatment with adder anti-venom.

Bee and wasp stings

Painful, but usually single and with no serious general effects, insect stings require little more than removal of the sting itself in the case of bee stings (wasps and hornets do not leave their stings behind) by means of tweezers and the application of antihistamine cream. Rarely, death can ensue if a dog is subject to a large number, perhaps hundreds, of stings. Stings can also be serious if the tongue or mouth are involved.

Common symptoms
The dog's throat will swell, or, if he is allergic to the insect venom, he will go into severe shock.

Recommended action
If your dog goes into shock, he will need anti-shock therapy, such as intravenous fluids, adrenalin and antihistamine injections. Keep him warm and make sure that his breathing is unimpeded while you obtain veterinary attention.

Bleeding

The appearance of blood anywhere on a dog's body necessitates immediate close inspection. A variety of accidents and some diseases may produce blood from the nostrils, eyes or ears or in the droppings or in vomited material. None of the above types of haemorrhage are usually suitable for first aid by the owner. All need veterinary attention, however, though the causes may often be trivial and ephemeral.

Bleeding from the body surface through wounds inflicted during fights, traffic accidents or other traumatic incidents can be copious, and this does require prompt first aid.

Recommended action

The most important thing you can do is to apply pressure to the wound. Hand or finger pressure is always invaluable until a pad of gauze or cotton wool can be found. This should be soaked in cold water, placed on the wound and kept in place by constant firm pressure or, better still, a bandage. Take the dog to a veterinary surgery as quickly as possible. Do not waste any time applying antiseptic ointments or powders to a significantly bleeding wound.

Heat stroke

Every summer we read in the newspapers of cases of dogs dying from heat stroke as a result of the gross thoughtlessness and negligence of their owners. Just like babies and young children, dogs who are left in hot, poorly ventilated spaces, particularly cars, and sometimes without water, will overheat. They lose the ability to control their internal body temperature. As the latter rises, the dog will become distressed, pant rapidly and will quickly weaken. His mouth will appear much redder than normal. Collapse, coma and even death can follow in a reasonably short space of time, so you must act quickly.

Recommended action

Cooling the affected dog's body, particularly his head, by means of cold water baths, hosing and ice packs is essential. If the temperature-regulating mechanism in the brain has already been seriously damaged a fatal outcome may still ensue. Veterinary attention must be obtained immediately. Of course, by being a responsible and thoughtful owner, you can prevent such emergencies occurring.

Soak the bandage in cold water before applying it to the wound, then seek veterinary treatment as soon as possible if the bleeding does not stop.

A dog with suspected heat stroke must be hosed down with plenty of cold water immediately. You may also need to use ice packs.

Foreign bodies

These can occur in various parts of a dog's anatomy
and treatment will vary according to the location.

In the eye

Foreign bodies in the eye will cause the dog to rub
his head on the ground and paw at his eye.

Recommended action

Flood the affected eye with human-type eye drops
or olive oil to float out the foreign body. Do not use
tweezers close to the eyeball.

In the ear

Plant seeds and grass awns are particularly likely to
get into a dog's ears during summer walks. Their
presence causes itching and irritation. The dog will
shake his head and scratch and paw at his ears.

Recommended action

Pour warm olive oil or other vegetable oil into the ear,
filling it. The object may float to the surface and can
be picked up by tweezers. Deeper, embedded foreign
bodies will always require veterinary attention.

In the mouth

Pieces of bone or splinters of wood can become
lodged in a dog's mouth. The offending object may
be jammed between the left and right upper molars
at the back of the mouth or between two adjacent
teeth. Less commonly, an object, such as a small
ball, gets stuck in a dog's throat. In all cases, he will
show symptoms of distress, including pawing at the
mouth, gagging, trying to retch or shaking his head.

Recommended action

While someone holds the dog firmly, you should open his mouth and try to dislodge the foreign body with a spoon or kitchen tongs. Where the dog is having difficulty breathing and literally choking, try holding him upside down, massaging the throat and slapping his back. If you cannot remove the object, you must seek veterinary help at once.

In the paws

Splinters of glass, thorns, particles of metal and even fragments of stone can penetrate the pads on a dog's paws or lodge in the skin between the toes. As a result, the dog limps and usually licks the affected paw.

Recommended action

If the object is visible, you can remove it with tweezers. If not, because of being embedded, then bathe the foot two to three times daily in warm water and salt (a teaspoon to a cupful) until the foreign body emerges from the softened skin. If lameness persists for more than a day or two, seek veterinary attention as infection may set in.

After removing a foreign object from a paw, bathe it in warm salty water. Do likewise if you can't remove it straight away as this may help the object appear.

A grass seed between the dog's pads can be very painful. Use some tweezers to pull it out but check the seed is still complete.

Resuscitating a dog

If your dog's heart fails as the result of an accident, convulsion or drowning, you must try to resuscitate him, either by cardiac massage or artificial respiration. Check his airway is clear first.

Check breathing and heart rate

If the dog is unconscious, you must find out whether he is still breathing as well as assessing his heart action. To check for signs of life, feel for a heart beat (as illustrated below) and watch for the rise and fall of the chest wall. Check that his airway is clear and the breathing is not obstructed by any blood, saliva or vomit in his throat.

1 You should feel for the dog's pulse on the inside of a hind leg.

2 Press the flat of your hand against the dog's chest just behind the elbow.

3 Place your ear on the dog's chest to listen for heart beats. Normal respiration rate is 20–30 breaths per minute. Normal heart rate ranges from about 50 beats per minute in large breeds to 150 beats per minute in very small breeds.

Cardiac massage

If you cannot hear or feel the dog's heart beating you should try cardiac massage by doing the following.

• Put the dog on his right side with the heel of your left hand on the left side of his chest behind the elbow.

• Put your other hand on top and then press down and forwards firmly and sharply.

• Do this 10 times at regular one-second intervals.

Mouth-to-nose resuscitation

Assuming that the dog is not breathing, you should now give mouth-to-nose resuscitation.

• Maintain an airway by clearing obstructions or saliva from the dog's mouth and pulling the tongue forwards, allowing it to flop out to one side.

• Keep his head and neck straight and, cupping the nose with your hands, breathe out strongly into the nostrils for two to three seconds. The chest should expand as the lungs fill with air.

• If the heart is still not beating, do cardiac massage 10 times and then do artificial respiration again.

• Continue alternating the massage and the mouth-to-nose until you get a response. It is worth trying for up to 15 minutes to re-start the heart, and artificial respiration should continue indefinitely where a faint heart beat can be detected.

Put one hand on top of the other and press down and forwards, firmly and sharply.

Keep the dog's head and neck straight and then, cupping his nose with your hands, you must exhale strongly into his nostrils.

want to know more?

• The PDSA (People's Dispensary for Sick Animals) provides free veterinary care for pets owned by people on low incomes at their clinics: tel: 01952 290 999 www.pdsa.org.uk

weblinks

• To find a vet in your area, you can log on to the website of the Royal College of Veterinary Surgeons at www.rcvs.org.uk
• For the British Veterinary Association: www.bva.co.uk

Need to know more?

Useful organizations

Animal Samaritans
PO Box 154
Bexleyheath
Kent DA16 2WS
tel: 020 8698 0357
www.animalsamaritans.co.uk

**Association of Pet
Behaviour Counsellors**
PO Box 46
Worcester WR8 9YS
tel: 01386 751151
www.apbc.org.uk

**Association of Pet Dog
Trainers**
Peacocks Farm
Northchapel, Petworth
West Sussex GU28 9JB
tel: 01285 810811
www.apdt.co.uk

Battersea Dogs' Home
4 Battersea Park Road
Battersea
London SW8 4AA
tel: 020 7622 3626
www.dogshome.org

Blue Cross
Shilton Road
Burford
Oxon OX18 4PF
tel: 01993 822651
www.bluecross.org.uk

**British Veterinary
Association**
7 Mansfield Street
London W1M 0AT
tel: 020 7636 6541
www.bva.co.uk

DEFRA
Information Resource Centre
Lower Ground Floor
Ergon House
c/o Nobel House
17 Smith Square
London SW1P 3JR
tel: 020 7238 6951
www.defra.gov.uk

**Jay Gee Animal Sanctuary
for Dogs**
Head Office
Broughton
Brigg
North Lincolnshire DN20 0BJ
tel: 01652 653343
www.jerrygreen.org.uk

**PDSA
(People's Dispensary for
Sick Animals)**
PDSA House
Whitechapel Way
Priorslee
Telford
Shropshire TF2 9PQ
tel: 01952 290 999
www.pdsa.org.uk

Pet Care Trust
Bedford Business Centre
170 Mile Road
Bedford MK42 9TW
tel: 08700 624400
email: info@petcare.org.uk
www.petcare.org.uk

Puppy School
PO Box 186
Chipping Norton
Oxon OX7 3XG
tel: 01608 676931
www.puppyschool.co.uk

**Royal College of Veterinary
Surgeons**
62–64 Horseferry Road
London SW1P 2AF
tel: 020 7222 2001
www.rcvs.org.uk

RSPCA
Causeway
Horsham
West Sussex RH12 1HG
tel: 0870 55 55 999
(cruelty and advice line)
tel: 0870 33 35 999
(enquiries service)
www.rspca.org.uk

The Kennel Club
1–5 Clarges Street
Piccadilly
London W1Y 8AB
tel: 0870 606 6750
email: info@the-kennel-
club.org.uk
www.the-kennel-club.org.uk

Useful websites

Cinnamon Trust
www.cinnamon.org.uk
Charity for elderly pet
owners, with dog walkers
and fostering.

Dog Aid Society of Scotland
www.dogaidsociety.com
Registered charity rehoming
dogs.

Dogs Trust
www.dogstrust.org.uk
UK's largest dog welfare
charity with rehoming and
rescue centres.

Greyhound Rescue
www.greyhoundrescue.co.uk
Greyhound rescue and
adoption in UK and Europe.

Mango Mutt
www.mangomutt.co.uk
Natural dog accessories.

Mayhew Animal Home
www.mayhewanimalhome.org
Animal home and education
and training centre.

**National Animal Welfare
Trust**
www.nawt.org.uk
Rescue centres around UK.

Pet Health Care
www.pethealthcare.co.uk
Online source of useful petcare
information.

Pet Organic
www.petorganic.com
Organic and natural petfoods.

Pet Planet
www.petplanet.co.uk
Wide range of products and
online shopping for pets.

Pets as Therapy (PAT)
www.petsastherapy.org
Hospital visiting scheme
in which dogs visit sick
and elderly.

UK Animal Rescuers
www.animalrescuers.co.uk
Guide to animal
welfare organizations,
rescue centres and
rehoming.

Magazines

Dog World
Somerfield House
Wotton Road
Ashford
Kent TN23 6LW
tel: 01233 621877
www.dogworld.co.uk

Dogs Monthly
Ascot House
High Street, Ascot
Berkshire SL5 7JG
tel: 0870 730 8433
www.dogsmonthly.co.uk

Dogs Today
Town Mill, Bagshot Road
Chobham
Surrey GU24 8BZ
tel: 01276 858860
www.dogstodaymagazine.co.uk

Our Dogs
5 Oxford Road
Station Approach
Manchester M60 1SX
Tel: 0161 236 2660
www.ourdogs.co.uk

Your Dog BPG (Stamford) Ltd
33 Broad Street
Stamford
Lincolnshire PE9 1RB
tel: 01780 766199
www.yourdog.co.uk

Further reading

Alderton, David, *How to Talk with Your Dog* (Collins)
Bailey, Gwen, *Collins Gem – Dog Training* (Collins)
Bailey, Gwen, *Dogs Behaving Badly: A Practical
    Problem Solver* (Collins)
Bailey, Gwen, *Puppy Handbook* (Collins)
Fisher, John, *Think Dog* (Cassell)
Fogle, Bruce, *The Encyclopedia of the Dog*
    (Dorling Kindersley)

Killick, Robert, *Dog Showing* (Collins)
RSPCA Pet Guide, *Collins Care for Your Dog*
    (Collins)
RSPCA Pet Guide, *Collins Care for Your Puppy*
    (Collins)
Smyth, Stella, and Bergh-Roose, Sally, *need to
    know? Dog Training* (Collins)
Stilwell, Victoria, *It's Me or the Dog* (Collins)

Index

Afghan Hound 146
aggressive behaviour 40, 43, 56, 117, 134–135
American Cocker Spaniel 146
anxious behaviour 40, 116, 124–125
arthritis 120, 170, 171
bad breath 74, 148, 154
barking 109
Basset Hound 46, 171
bathing 73
Battersea Dogs' Home 18, 21
Beagle 146, 147
'bed' 101
bedding 24, 26
bleeding 182–183
blood in stools 165
boarding kennels 80
body language 116–117
bones 31, 62, 75
Border Collie 111, 146, 147
boredom 126
Boston Terrier 147
Boxer 13, 111, 146
breeders 14, 16
breed(s) 10–13, 14
  classification 10
  clubs 16
  standards 142
bronchitis 163
Bull Terrier 111, 147
Bulldog 73, 146
Bullmastiff 68
burns 178–179
calculi 168
car travel 48–49, 78, 136–137
cardiac massage 187
cardiovascular disease 146
cataract 146, 156
cats 31, 38, 132
Cavalier King Charles Spaniel 13
chasing 52, 132–133
cherry eye 146
chews 24, 31, 62, 75, 123, 126

Chihuahua 65
chocolate 61
Chow Chow 70
claws 76, 141, 148
Clumber Spaniel 146
Cocker Spaniel 13
Collies 52, 69, 111, 146, 149
'come' 92–93
commands 84
communicating with dogs 104–106
constipation 165
coughing 162, 163
counter-signing 114
crates 48–49
cross-breeds 17
cystitis 168
Dachshund 46, 171
Dalmatian 13, 111, 147
Dangerous Dogs Act 57
dangers 44–47
deafness 111, 147
destructive behaviour 40, 119, 126
diabetes 167
diarrhoea 31, 162, 164, 165, 166, 167
diet 24, 28–31, 60–63
distemper 156, 162, 164
Dobermann 13, 68, 146, 147
Dogs Trust 18, 21
'down' 94–95
'drop' 100
ears 50, 60, 71, 72, 74, 77, 110, 112, 116, 141, 142, 148, 158–160, 184
ectropion 146
elbow dysplasia 146
elderly dogs 79, 111, 120, 170
English Setter 147
English Springer Spaniel 13, 146, 149
entropion 146, 157
escaping 128
exercise 55, 64–65, 149

eyes 76, 112, 141, 146, 148, 156–157, 184
fearfulness 40, 116
feeding 12, 24, 27, 28–31, 60–63, 74, 79, 80, 135, 149, 164, 170
feet 76, 148, 184
'fetch' 98–99
'find' 101
first aid 142, 178–187
flatulence 166
fleas 140, 148, 150–151
foreign bodies 184–185
fouling public places 57
games 52–54, 64–65, 131, 133, 148
genetic tests 14, 144, 145
German Shepherd Dog 13, 68, 110, 134, 144, 146, 157
German Short-haired Pointer 146
glaucoma 146
Golden Retriever 66, 146, 147
good behaviour 26, 102–137
grass seeds 76, 148, 159
Great Dane 60, 146
Greyhound 18
grooming 12, 66–73, 173
gum disease 74, 155
gundogs 10, 65
hazards 44–47
healthcare 138–187
hearing 110–111
heart disease 163
heart rate 186
heat stroke 79, 183
hereditary diseases 144–147
'hi five' 101
hip dysplasia 14, 73, 144–145, 146, 170
hormonal diseases 147
hot spots 173
Hounds 10, 65, 73, 132

house soiling 120–121
house-training 32, 34–37, 120–121
identification 57
infectious canine hepatitis 164
insurance 51
Irish Setter 146
Irish Wolfhound 46, 55
Jack Russell Terrier 70
jumping up 130
Kennel Club 10, 14, 16, 18, 21, 142
kennel cough 163
Kerry Blue Terrier 68, 147, 158
kidney disease 167
Labrador Retriever 11, 13, 144, 146, 157
lead training 55, 96–97
leptospirosis 164, 168
lice 151, 172
lifting 177
Lurcher 18
Lyme Disease 152
mange 172
mating 128
medicines, giving 175
micro-chipping 57
mites 158
mongrels 17
moulting 67
mouth-to-mouth resuscitation 187
muzzle 176
nervous behaviour 43
neutering 14, 128
Newfoundland 146
nose 141, 148, 161, 162
obesity 60, 61, 149, 170
Old English Sheepdog 70, 147
osteochondrosis dessicans 146
pack leader 106
parasites 150–153, 172, 173
Parson Jack Russell Terrier 13
parvovirus infection 165
pastoral group 10, 65
Pekingese 65, 76, 171
Pet Travel Scheme 80–81
play 52–54, 64–65, 131
    biting 123

playpens 26–27, 125
pneumonia 163
poisonous plants 45, 180
poisons 44, 180–181
polydipsia 167
polyphagia 167
Pomeranian 65, 146
Poodle 13, 67, 71, 146, 147, 158
Pug 65, 67, 76, 112, 149, 156
puppies 22–57, 124–125
    bedding 26–27, 32
    car travel 48–49
    choosing 15
    collecting 24
    equipment 24
    exercising 55
    feeding 24, 27, 28–31
    grooming 67
    house-training 32, 34–37
    night-time 32–33
    other pets 38–39
    play and games 52–54
    play biting 123
    socializing 27, 38–39, 40–43
    training 84–101
    visiting the vet 50–51
puppy farms 16
rescue dogs 18–21, 124
resuscitation 186–187
Retrievers 11, 13, 53, 66, 144, 146
retrieving 52, 98–99
rewarding good behaviour 26, 86, 119
rhinitis 161
ringworm 172
roaming 128
rolling 115
Rottweiler 13, 144
Rough Collie 70, 147
St Bernard 146
salmonella 167
scent 114–115
    marking 121
scooting 153
scratching 150, 151, 158
separation anxiety 124–125
Shar Pei 68, 146
Shetland Sheepdog 146

Shih Tzu 69
sight 112
sinusitis 161
'sit' 88–89
skeletal diseases 146, 170–171
skin problems 60, 172–173
slipped disk 171
small pets 39
sneezing 161, 162
socialization 27, 38–39, 40–43, 134
    classes 42
Spaniels 13, 52, 53, 72, 74, 148, 159
spaying 14
stairgates 33, 46
'stay' 90–91
stings 182
submission 117
tablets, giving 175
tail docking 117
teeth 31, 74–75, 123, 141, 148, 154–155
temperature, taking 174–175
Terriers 10, 13, 53, 65, 71, 73, 115
territory marking 32, 47, 114
ticks 151–152, 172
toy group 10, 35, 65
toys 24, 54, 123, 126, 133
training 82–101
    lead training 55
travel boxes 48–49
travelling 78
urinary disease 168
utility group 10, 65
vaccinations 26, 40, 42, 50–51, 80, 168
veterinary surgery 43, 50–51
vocalization 108–109
vomiting 164, 165, 167
water 27, 31, 61, 167
weight 31, 60, 61, 140, 149, 166
Welsh Terrier 71
West Highland White Terrier 13
wolves 104–105
working group 10, 65, 149
worming 75, 149, 152–153
Yorkshire Terrier 13, 69

☼ Collins need to know?

Look out for these recent titles in Collins' practical and accessible need to know? series.

Other titles in the series:

Antique Marks	Decorating	How to Lose Weight	Speak Italian
Aquarium Fish	Detox	Kama Sutra	Speak Spanish
Birdwatching	Digital Photography	Kings and Queens	Stargazing
Body Language	DIY	Knots	Watercolour
Buying Property in France	Dog Training	Low GI/GL Diet	Weddings
Buying Property in Spain	Drawing & Sketching	Mushroom Hunting	Wine
Calorie Counting	Dreams	Pilates	Woodworking
Card Games	First Aid	Poker	The World
Chess	Food Allergies	Pregnancy	Universe
Children's Parties	Golf	Property	Yoga
Codes & Ciphers	Guitar	Speak French	Zodiac Types

To order any of these titles, please telephone 0870 787 1732 quoting reference 263H. For further information about all Collins books, visit our website: www.collins.co.uk